Gender

AIM HIGHER WITH *PALGRAVE INSIGHTS IN PSYCHOLOGY*

Also available in this series:

978-0-230-24986-8

978-0-230-27222-4

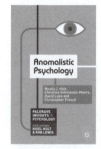

978-0-230-30150-4

978-0-230-24988-2

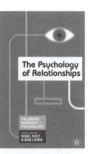

978-0-230-24941-7

978-0-230-25265-3

978-0-230-29537-7

Intelligence and Learning

978-0-230-24944-8

Sport Psychology

978-0-230-24987-5

Forensic Psychology

978-0-230-24942-4

978-0-230-29640-4

Health Psychology

978-0-230-24945-5

Phobias

978-0-230-29536-0

Gender

978-0-230-30273-0

To find out more visit **www.palgrave.com/insights**

Gender

Leanne Franklin

PALGRAVE INSIGHTS IN PSYCHOLOGY

SERIES EDITORS:
NIGEL HOLT
& ROB LEWIS

palgrave
macmillan

First published 2012 by
PALGRAVE MACMILLAN

Palgrave Macmillan in the UK is an imprint of Macmillan Publishers Limited, registered in England, company number 785998, of Houndmills, Basingstoke, Hampshire RG21 6XS.

Palgrave Macmillan in the US is a division of St Martin's Press LLC, 175 Fifth Avenue, New York, NY 10010.

Palgrave Macmillan is the global academic imprint of the above companies and has companies and representatives throughout the world.

Palgrave® and Macmillan® are registered trademarks in the United States, the United Kingdom, Europe and other countries.

ISBN 978–0–230–30273–0

This book is printed on paper suitable for recycling and made from fully managed and sustained forest sources. Logging, pulping and manufacturing processes are expected to conform to the environmental regulations of the country of origin.

A catalogue record for this book is available from the British Library.

A catalog record for this book is available from the Library of Congress.

10   9   8   7   6   5   4   3   2   1
21 20 19 18 17 16 15 14 13 12

Printed and bound in China

For my family – especially my fiancé whose support made this project possible and my mum as a thank you for her constant encouragement and pride

Contents

Tables

Note from series editors

The development of gender is a fascinating topic, and one that has animated psychologists for some time. For most readers, it is not even immediately clear what gender is and how it might be defined. Here, the topic has been addressed clearly, leaving no confusion.

We were very pleased that Leanne agreed to take on this book. She is a person with energy, wide interests and a number of areas of expertise, which together make a formidable academic. On top of this, it became clear early on that she writes with vision and clarity, and although we as editors were careful to direct her coverage in small part, she clearly took up the ball and ran with it, and her enthusiasm shines through. The result which you see here is a well-formed, pragmatic approach that fits perfectly in the series and which we are certain will provide those who read it with the insight they are looking for.

- *If you are reading this book as a preparation for university study* you will find material relevant to a range of disciplines within psychology and elsewhere. A good overview of this topic is essential for those preparing for topics where human development or social and personal perspectives are important or relevant, from psychology to education, sociology to childcare.
- *If reading this book while at university* it is likely that you are undertaking a course focused on or featuring the study of human development. It is the nature of psychology that it has relevance beyond its academically prescribed boundaries, and students of a range of topics will find this book informative and useful. The way

Leanne has written the book allows people to approach the topic from a range of perspectives and we hope you will find it useful.

- *If you are reading the book as part of a pre-university course, such as an A-level,* you will have found some of the material in this book mentioned in your textbooks and in your specification guidelines. What Leanne has done is to include an up-to-date, professional academic's perspective on these issues and she has extended them to provide you with the necessary detail to help you really focus and perform as well as you possibly can in the examinations. You'll find a table in the Reading Guide, which will direct you to places in the book that you'll find most useful.

This book is part of a successful series that draws on the knowledge and skills of academics around the UK and further afield. We chose the author carefully and are delighted with the book you hold in your hands. Whatever the reason for reading this book, be it as part of your studies or just because you find it interesting, and perhaps relevant to your own lives, we have no doubt you will find it informative and useful. We are very pleased to add it to our series.

NIGEL HOLT AND ROB LEWIS
Series Editors

Chapter 1

Introduction

This opening chapter will outline the shape of the rest of the book. To begin with however it is essential that we understand what we mean when we refer to 'gender'. This book will primarily be concerned with gender, rather than sex. Sex refers to the biological and reproductive classification of an organism – male or female. Gender, on the other hand, refers to the cultural aspect of sex – how we come to know ourselves as social beings that are male and female. This is a distinction that has been widely adopted within psychology, but it is important to acknowledge the particular academic background from which this distinction first emerged.

This differentiation is somewhat taken for granted in social sciences today, but it is in fact a relatively recent shift in thinking that came about in the 1960s and early 1970s as a new wave of feminism took hold and academics began to challenge the long-held assumptions about sex and gender. Ground-breaking writers such as Simone de Beauvoir and Anne Oakley began to challenge the assumption that gender was a certainty of nature and not socially constructed. One of de Beauvoir's most influential ideas was that 'one is not born, but rather becomes a woman'. This shift in thinking became known as the '**sex/gender binary**' and the central presuppositions of this binary can be seen below:

THE SEX/GENDER BINARY (Taken from Richardson, 2008, p. 5):

- A distinction can be made between sex (biology) and gender (culture).
- Sex is biologically given and universal.
- Gender is historically and culturally variable.
- Sex consists of two – and only two – types of human beings.
- This two-sex model of sexual differences (the distinction between females and males) is a natural 'fact of life'.
- One sex in every body.
- Identities develop as either one or other of these two sexes/genders.

There has been a debate as to whether this differentiation remains useful as there is an argument that the biological body itself is socially constructed and so a differentiation between biology (sex) and the social (gender) is a fallacy. However, for clarity of understanding for the student reader, the terms gender (as social) and sex (as biological) will be used carefully (for those interested in this debate Hird (2000) provides a useful introduction to this area). This differentiation between sex and gender will be adopted for the purposes of this text and these definitions will be used throughout.

This book seeks to understand how we come to be these gendered beings and how we come to know ourselves as men and women within contemporary British culture. In Chapter 2 we will address the biological basis of our genders and explore the biology of the sexes. We will look at how we become male and female beings, both in the womb and during **adolescence**; we are obviously born as male or female but our sexes become more differentiated during our teenage years as we progress through **puberty**. We will also look at cases where this differentiation is not clear and the limitations of only having a male/female binary will become clear.

In Chapters 3–5 of the book we will take a chronological look at gender through childhood. Newborn male and female babies are much the same, both are driven by their biological requirements; however, by the time the child reaches 18 gender differences are clear; so it is worth exploring how these changes occur. In Chapter 3 we will look at the early years and focus on gender before the child reaches school age. At this point gender differences mainly come from external sources, from the clothes the child is dressed in or from parental reactions to gendered behaviour, and slowly the child begins to develop an understanding of what gender means. Once children begin school gendered behaviours become even more apparent and this is explored in Chapter 4. In this chapter we will focus on the primary school years (ages 4–11) and explore gender differences in **play** and in the classroom. We will also look at how gender impacts upon sibling relationships; while much literature focuses on parent–child relations the relationship between siblings is often overlooked but is very important in child development. In Chapter 5 we will move onto adolescence. The physical differences between the genders are detailed in Chapter 2, and so this chapter will focus upon the psychological changes and events associated with gender. We will look at peer relationships, with a particular focus on **bullying**, as friends become paramount during adolescence. We will also look at sexuality and gender differences in educational attainment as these are also issues that come to the fore during this period of life.

Once we have explored the effects of gender during childhood from a chronological perspective we will turn to psychological theories for an understanding of why these differences might occur and how our gendered identities develop. In Chapter 6 we will look to the work of Freud and Erikson in particular for an understanding of psychoanalytic perspectives of gender. In Chapter 7 we will then turn to an alternative perspective and to the work of Kohlberg for an appreciation of how gender is dependent upon cognitive development. In Chapter 8 we will look to the work of Bem to explore the **gender schema** approach and in Chapter 9 we will look to Bandura and social learning theory. All of these theoretical perspectives offer psychologists competing explanations as to how we become socialised into culturally acceptable forms of masculinity and femininity. In Chapter 10 we will look at the social constructionist perspective which suggests that the cultural and historical environments are crucial to how gender is constructed and consequently how gender develops during childhood.[1] These theories will provide an overview of the dominant psychological perspectives regarding gender development.

In the final chapters we will draw attention to how gender is socially constructed and culturally specific by looking at alternative notions of what it means to be a woman and man. In Chapter 11 this will be done by looking at historical notions of gender from the United Kingdom. We will look to Christianity to understand the fundamental concepts of masculinity and femininity that have shaped the lives of British men and women for centuries. We will then track changes in gender equality during a relatively recent historical period that has been witness to the suffrage movement and several waves of feminism. Finally in the last chapter we will look to other cultures to better understand how gender occurs in other societies. We will look to India and the preference for sons which means that female foetuses may not even get the chance of life. We will then move to Africa and the phenomena of female genital mutilation and the HIV/AIDS crisis to see how a vast proportion of the population is suffering due to traditional notions of gender and sexuality. Finally we will look to the Mosuo in China which represents the most matriarchal society in the contemporary world to understand that there are alternative concepts of gender.

Throughout this book the primary focus will be on contemporary British culture: however, at times research from America will be introduced. America is the leading producer of psychological research and so it would be very difficult to produce a text that only included research from Britain. Thus while the focus will predominantly be on the United Kingdom, much of what will be discussed will be applicable to western society in general.

Chapter 2

Sex differences

This chapter will address the biological basis of gender: sex. Our socialisation into gender-appropriate roles begins when our sex is identified, whether prenatally or at the moment of birth. This chapter will describe the biological development of sex from within the womb to the completion of our mature sexual form, which occurs during adolescence. The chapter will end with an examination of how we come to know our gendered bodies; that is, how sex determines how we are socialised into understanding and experiencing our corporeal forms.

In this chapter we will address the following points:

- The prenatal development of gender, including a brief exploration of **Turner's Syndrome** and **hermaphroditism**
- The process of puberty, including a closer look at sex
- The experience of **gender dysphoria**, which will be illustrated with an exploration of **transsexualism** and the case study of Joan/John
- The chapter will end with an examination of how culture and biology are interrelated, with a particular focus on *fa'afafine* to demonstrate how culture and biology are entwined

The genetic basis of sex

Genes are the building blocks of our body and the sex of an individual is fundamentally determined by their genes. The human body normally has 23 pairs of genes, with one half of each pair being contributed by each parent. The gene pair that determines gender is either XX (female) or XY (male). All ova, the reproductive cell of the mother, contain the X chromosome. Sperm, the reproductive cell (or gamete) of the father, contains either a Y or an X chromosome, and so it is this paternal contribution to the genetic structure that determines sex. Thus the sex of a child is determined by the genes carried by the sperm; an ovum fertilised by a sperm containing an X chromosome will develop into a female and those fertilised by a sperm carrying a Y chromosome will be male.

Developing zygotes (this term refers to the newly fertilised gametes) are identical until six weeks after conception, at which point the gonads (or sex organs) become specific to the sexes. In males this is determined by genetic coding on the Y chromosome and the gonads develop into testes; whereas in females the gonads later develop into ovaries. Forty-two days after conception the sex differences in the embryo become visible; up until this point the developing embryos look alike regardless of sex, and once this point has been passed, new parents are able to find out the sex of their new child via ultrasound. It is the presence (or absence) of external sex organs that determines sex identification, either by an ultrasound during pregnancy or immediately after birth. It is therefore the **sexual dimorphism** (physical differences between men and women) at birth that determines the ascribed sex of the child. However, assumption of sex based on genitalia can be problematic as in the case of Turner's Syndrome and for those individuals born as hermaphrodites.

Turner's Syndrome

Turner's Syndrome is a rare condition which occurs when the developing zygote does not have a second sex chromosome (the additional X or Y chromosome received from the sperm). The syndrome was first identified in the 1930s (Turner, 1938) and in 1996 (Saenger) it was estimated that there were between 50,000 and 75,000 individuals with the syndrome. Those individuals with Turner's Syndrome possess female external genitalia, but frequently lack internal female gonads. Females with this condition also experience a number of other developmental irregularities which might affect finger nails, kidneys, the skeletal system and height. However there are treatments available, most notably hormone therapy, which stimulate development of secondary sexual characteristics and which are designed to target individual aspects of the condition (such as calcium supplements to prevent bone deterioration). Fertility treatments also mean that pregnancy can be an option for those women with Turner's Syndrome and a fertilisation rate of 50–60 per cent has been reported (Saenger, 1996).

Turner's Syndrome is of interest to those studying gender because those affected individuals are neither XX (female) nor XY (male), but a third gender (XO) (Unger & Crawford, 1996). This identification of a third gender is problematic for the 'sex/gender binary', which clearly identifies only two sexes: male and female. Those individuals with Turner's Syndrome demonstrate that the demarcation between male and female is not as simple as first believed, but is rather more blurred than one might initially believe.

Intersex individuals (hermaphrodites)

Hermaphrodite was a Greek demi-god and the son of Hermes (god of male sexuality) and Aphrodite (goddess of love). Salmacis, a nymph, fell in love and desired to forever be a part of him, and from this point Hermaphrodite was half male and half female. Although this is a tale from Greek mythology the name has remained in our vernacular and the term is now used to refer to anyone who is born with intersex genitalia (genitals of both males and females). In the Victorian era there was a definition made between pseudo-hermaphrodites and true-hermaphrodites. True hermaphrodites are those individuals who possess functioning male and female genitalia and reproductive organs. Pseudo-hermaphrodites, on the other hand, may develop aspects of both male and female sexual organs, but these gonads are non-functional (i.e. not capable of reproduction).

Today such individuals are known as 'intersex' by the medical community, but this implies a type of limbo for those individuals: they are neither one, nor the other. Fausto-Sterling (1993) suggested an additional three sexes based on hermaphroditism:

Herms: Traditionally known as true hermaphrodites who possess at least one ovary and one testis.

Merms: Male pseudo-hermaphrodites who have testes, some aspects of female genitalia, but no ovaries.

Ferms: Female pseudo-hermaphrodites who have ovaries, no testes, but some aspects of male genitalia.

These suggestions have clearly not been adopted into mainstream use, but do provide us with an alternative way of perceiving gender; that is more as a continuum, rather than a binary.

There are suggestions that approximately 2 per cent of live births are ambiguous, that is intersex individuals that are not clearly either male or female (Blackless et al., 2000). However, the majority of these are due to genital abnormalities that do not require surgical intervention and it is just 0.1–0.2 per cent of these births that require surgical intervention (ibid.). However, Fautsto-Sterling (2000a) also reports that these figures are variable across cultures and uses the example of Congenital Adrenal Hyperplasia (CAH). This is a genetic condition whereby the affected child possesses XX chromosomes (genetically female), develops female internal organs (which may be reproductively functional), but has male external genitals. In certain populations this gene is more prevalent: for example, among the Yupik Eskimo it has a frequency of 3500 per million, but in New Zealand this frequency drops to 43 per million (ibid.). Thus CAH and the associated intersex condition is more common where this genetic frequency is higher.

There is currently debate in the medical and social sciences about how to best support or treat those individuals born as hermaphrodites or with genitals that are ambiguous. There are currently surgical attempts to 'normalise' these individuals and to offer cosmetic intervention to change these genitals into recognisably male or female organs. However this is complicated by disagreement over what constitutes 'normal' genitalia at birth; Fausto-Sterling (2000b) provides a comprehensive discussion of such debates, regarding both male and female genitalia. There is now a call for offering hermaphrodites and intersex individuals no surgical intervention during infancy but to offer guidance and counselling to the individual before allowing them to make up their own mind (Dreger, 1998; Fausto-Sterling, 2000a; Kessler, 1998). This is countered by some researchers and clinicians however (e.g. Slijper et al., 1998) who recommend gender (re)assignment at birth.

⊙ The influence of hormones

Puberty is the period of sexual maturation when biologically immature children develop into reproductively capable adults. The onset of puberty in both sexes is triggered by the release of gonadotropic hormones (follicle stimulating hormone (FSH) and luteinising hormone (LH)) from the pituitary gland. However, what causes the release of these hormones and consequently the onset of puberty is something of a medical mystery as researchers are still unable to identify what triggers this aspect of the developmental clock (Sisk & Foster, 2004). Puberty usually begins between the ages of 10 and 16, although girls begin puberty a year or two earlier than boys and can begin this stage of development as young as eight. There has been a decrease in the onset age of adolescence which is referred to as a secular trend, which has been caused by changes in nutrition over the last century. It should be noted that all three of the hormones we shall be focusing on are found in both men and women: therefore **testosterone** is not a solely male hormone, and **oestrogen** and **progesterone** not solely female hormones.

Oestrogen and progesterone fall within a group of hormones that are called 'estradiols', which refer to sex hormones mainly found in women. Oestrogen is one of the two predominant hormones in female bodies (the other, progesterone, is described next), is produced by the ovaries and is responsible for changes during puberty and development of secondary sexual characteristics, such as the growth of breasts. It is also important in the strengthening of bones and also works to protect blood vessels and the heart; furthermore it acts to control fatty deposits around the body, particularly around the hips, giving women their curvaceous bodies. Progesterone is produced during the second half of the reproductive cycle by the ovaries and is particularly important during the reproductive cycle as it prepares the womb to accept a fertilised egg. Progesterone (and synthetic variations) is also very important in hormonal contraception, such as the contraceptive pill.

Testosterone is the hormone that is typically associated with men and is one of a larger group of hormones called androgens. It is a form of anabolic steroid which is produced in the testes and adrenal glands. In an adult man it is important in the production of sperm, whereas in the adolescent boy it is crucial in the maturation of sex organs and the development of secondary sexual characteristics, such as facial hair. Testosterone is also associated with certain traits, particularly aggressiveness (Archer, 1991; Book et al., 2001). We will now turn to the process of puberty; the effects of puberty on each sex differ and will be discussed below as we will explore males and females separately.

Puberty in males

Puberty in males is a gradual process with changes to both the primary organs and the development of secondary sexual characteristics. First we will explore changes to the sexual organs and then move on to the secondary changes. Male puberty begins with the development of testes which is visibly noticeable by the growth of the testes and changes to the scrotal sac (in size and colour); the penis will also undergo changes at this time and grow in both length and width. In addition the testes will lower as this reduces the temperature of the scrotum which aids the production of sperm. Although erections can occur throughout life, it is at this stage that they become more frequent. During puberty a boy can expect to experience several erections a day, often unrelated to sexual desire, but due to the physical changes his body is undergoing. At puberty males also develop the ability to ejaculate which often happens at night during a 'wet dream'. Once ejaculations begin men are physically capable of reproduction.

The most noticeable physical changes during puberty (for both boys and girls) are the development of secondary sexual characteristics. In boys this means the development of facial hair, the deepening of the voice and overall changes to the body shape and size. The presence of oestrogen in the body, which supports bone and muscle growth, means that boys undergo a rapid growth spurt, in both height and muscle mass. It is not only facial hair that develops at this time, but also pubic hair, armpit hair and perhaps chest hair. These changes are often unpredictable and can vary dramatically between individuals; just as every adult body is different so is the process of transition (i.e. puberty).

Puberty in females

In females the gonadotropic hormones act to stimulate production of hormones by the ovaries and these hormones act to stimulate breast development, deposition of body fat (such as around the hips) and growth of the uterine lining. Additional secondary sexual characteristics are stimulated by androgens which are released from the adrenal glands (located at the top of the kidneys) and these stimulate growth of pubic and axillary hair. The predominant change to female bodies that occurs during puberty is menstruation which marks the onset of reproductive ability. The age of first menstruation has been decreasing in western society in recent times due to improvements in health and nutrition and the average age currently stands at 13 years in the United Kingdom, although one in eight females starts menstruating before leaving primary school (i.e. at age 11) (Whincup et al., 2001).

The menstrual cycle is determined by the female hormones oestrogen and progesterone. This cycle follows an approximately monthly cycle, but the exact cycle length varies from woman to woman. At the beginning of this cycle the pituitary gland in the brain produces a follicle stimulating hormone (FSH) which is directed to a particular ovarian follicle. FSH acts upon the follicle to develop into its mature form, an ovum, and stimulates the production of oestrogen by the ovaries. It is oestrogen which causes the development of the womb lining and the process of ovulation (the release of the mature ovum from the ovaries). The follicle (from which the ovum was formed) also secretes the hormone progesterone which prepares the womb lining for the receipt of a zygote (should the ovum be fertilised). If fertilisation does not occur then the oestrogen and progesterone cease to be produced in such high quantities and the womb lining begins to disintegrate. It is this process of disintegration and loss of lining that is the monthly process of menstruation.

It is also worth mentioning Pre-Menstrual Syndrome (PMS) at this juncture which is caused by fluctuations in hormone levels during the menstrual cycle. This is a condition which affects 5–8 per cent of women severely enough that distress or impairment to daily functioning is caused (Yonkers et al., 2008), although some studies suggest that this figure could be as high as 20 per cent (Borenstein et al., 2003). Extreme experiences of PMS are diagnosed as Premenstrual Dysmorphic Disorder (PMDD) (American Psychiatric Association, 2000). Symptoms of PMS or PMDD include physical discomfort (such as bloating or tenderness), changes in appetite and energy patterns, and changes in mood (including irritability, anger and depression).

◉ Evolutionary perspectives on sex and gender

From a developmental perspective it may seem superfluous to examine why there are two reproductively capable sexes: males and females. Simply put the answer is reproduction. The presence of two sexes, male and female, means that reproduction is sexual, rather than asexual. Asexual reproduction is common among single-celled creatures, such as bacteria, and some other organisms, such as some plants and fungi. This type of reproduction involves a single organism reproducing a genetically identical offspring independently and without assistance; this enables very rapid reproduction and is capable of producing great numbers very quickly. It particularly benefits creatures that are not mobile; however, the greatest disadvantage this reproductive method presents is evolutionary development. As asexual organisms reproduce genetically identical offspring, the opportunity for evolution is extremely limited and these organisms can remain unchanged for millions of years, meaning that they are unable to adapt to changes in their environment.

Sexual reproduction, on the other hand, enables species to develop and evolve to better suit their environments. By combining genetic material with another, parents are able to create offspring that are genetically different from themselves, which allows greater opportunity for evolutionary development, genetic mutation and diversity. However, from a biological perspective there are advantages and disadvantages to sexual reproduction. It is much more costly in terms of time and effort required to have offspring, but these disadvantages are outweighed by the general benefits in terms of evolution. Sexual reproduction strictly refers to the exchange of genetic material between organisms, such as the exchange of pollen in plants, rather than the act of reproduction itself. In mammals two sexes have evolved in order to allow for reproduction and in humans the sexes show a great amount of sexual dimorphism, which may not be present in other animals.

In itself gender is a little explored area of research for evolutionary psychologists simply because they perceive gender to be a cultural and social construct: rather researchers investigate sex. One famous assumption of one aspect of evolutionary psychology is the 'mamawawa': the men are men and women are women assumption. This states that the differences between the sexes are fixed, are established prenatally and are based upon biological differences. However, there are some fundamental problems with this hypothesis which are pointed at towards the end of this chapter. Firstly the division between male and female is not black and white, but there are various shades of grey (such as in the case of Turner's Syndrome or gender dysphoria). Furthermore the categories of male and female are not mutually exclusive and it is possible for individuals to exhibit both masculine and feminine characteristics.

Evolutionary psychology argues that there are adaptive differences which meet the requirements of each sex; this means that there are some behaviours which are equally required by both sexes, therefore there may be no gender differences apparent. Perhaps the greatest variation between the sexes is reproductive behaviour which is based upon the different physical processes involved for each sex. It is argued that as men produce more gametes (i.e. sperm) than women they seek to copulate with as many potential mothers of offspring as possible, women however have less reproductive opportunities and so select a mate more carefully based on status and health; men are also likely to prefer younger women as this is an indication of fertility. This is supported by Buss (1994) who studied the mating preferences of over 10,000 people across six continents and reported that women make dating choices based on status and availability of resources, whereas men preferred women whose appearance indicated fertility. These mating preferences are reflected in experiences of jealousy, with women tending to display jealousy regarding emotional attachment whereas men are more likely to be jealous about physical encounters (Buss, 2000). There is also evidence that people in relationships with androgynous individuals, rather than feminine or masculine, report more satisfaction in their partnerships (Zammichieli et al., 1988), which is in opposition to the evolutionary hypothesis.

Thinking scientifically → **Nature/nurture debate and gender**

When thinking about the issue of nature/nurture with regards to gender it is impossible to clearly separate the two. Certainly there are many aspects to the 'nature' side of the debate: primarily experienced through our bodies. We are born as either male or female (apart from exceptional cases which are explored throughout this chapter) and we come to know ourselves and be known as male or female based on our corporeal form. It is not only the ostensible sex differences (such as facial hair) but also differences in genetic and hormonal make up.

However, how we come to know those bodies as gendered is clearly affected by our cultural and our social roles: it is nurtured. What it means to be a man or a woman is dictated by cultural norms and varies across time and space, and so we are brought up according to these cultural notions; imagine a woman growing up in the fifteenth century and how different her life would be to that of a woman brought up in the twenty-first century.

Perhaps the simplest way of looking at the nature/nurture debate is that our sex is natured, but our gender is nurtured.

Another area of research regarding sex and evolutionary psychology has been the differences that have been found in brain structure and functioning. The sexual dimorphism between men and women is easy to see, but there are also areas of difference that are not visible to the naked eye and which rely upon modern imaging techniques. Techniques such as positron emission tomography (PET), single photon emission computed tomography (SPECT) and functional magnetic resonance imaging (fMRI) have enabled researchers to develop an understanding of brain structure, function and composition in a way that was previously unattainable. In a 2007 review of literature Cosgrove, Mazure and Staley produced a meta-analysis of the differences such technology has yielded. They found that studies have consistently shown that the brain volume of females is 1,130cc, but that males have a volume of 1,260cc; however, women have a higher proportion of grey matter and men tend to have more white matter. Women also have more cerebral blood flow and display a generally higher level of cognitive activity.

Unsurprisingly given the structural differences outlined above there have also been differences found in areas of cognitive functioning. It has been consistently found that males score higher than females on tasks that involve mental rotation, spatial navigation and targeting (Baron-Cohen et al., 2005; Buss, 2012). On the other hand women are better at spatial location memory and also tend to score higher in object recognition (Buss, 2012). These differences in skills have led researchers (Silverman & Eals, 1992; Silverman & Philips, 1998) to suggest that this divergence is the result of historical sex roles; that is the hunter gatherer theory of spatial abilities. In essence this theory states that each sex has developed skills which assisted them in their roles as either hunters (males) or gatherers (females). Thus men perform better in skills that would assist in hunting, such as the ability to throw a spear accurately, and women have adapted to better recall the location of and to recognise objects, which would be useful skills when gathering plant foods. This hypothesis has received much support over the years and continues to be supported by empirical evidence.

However, evolutionary theories of gender differences have been criticised as being too simplistic, after all human society is much more evolved than animal communities and so the basis of choosing a mate is also more sophisticated; evolutionary psychology has also been accused of reinforcing and promoting traditional gender **stereotypes**. Furthermore it is also impossible to state whether the biological, behavioural or cognitive adaptation preceded the behaviour or vice versa: it is similar to trying to establish whether the chicken or the egg came first. It is impossible to ascertain whether men developed better mental rotation skills because of their habitual use of these abilities, or whether their superior mental rotation skills meant that they were adept at spear use. It has been shown that mental structures can change after periods of trauma or repeated practice of skills (Bremner et al., 1999; Münte et al., 2002). Thus while there is some evidence to suggest an evolutionary basis for differences between the sexes, there is also evidence to suggest that the human species has evolved beyond mere biology and that gender (as opposed to sex) is a matter of culture, not anatomy.

◉ Biosocial approaches to sex and gender

The biosocial approach to gender development suggests that both social and biological effects interact to produce a gendered being. It was first suggested by Money and Ehrhardt (1972) who theorised that there are a number of critical points in the child's gender development:

1 The first of these events is the receiving of an X or Y chromosome by the ovum. This exchange of a single cell has an unmistakable and crucial role to play in the future sex and gender development of the child. If an X chromosome is received then ovaries form and if a Y then testes develop.
2 The development of these gonads at around six weeks leads to the second crucial episode where the testes produce two hormones (testosterone and Müllerian-inhibiting substance) which prevent the development of female sexual organs. If these hormones are not present then the female reproductive system continues to develop.
3 At the third critical point, at approximately 12–16 weeks after conception, testosterone will continue to be produced and will cause the development of a penis and scrotum.
4 The next crucial step occurs after birth and is the labelling of the child's sex. As described earlier this classification is based on the appearance of the child's external genitalia at birth.
5 Finally biology takes precedence again during puberty when hormones lead to the development of an adult body, in terms of both reproductive capability and the appearance of secondary sexual characteristics.

The above list is predominantly made up of biological factors, but these are tempered by social reactions to biological events. An individual will react variably to the physical changes of puberty for example; the child will also face different reactions based on these changes, such as the difference in treatment between teenagers who seemingly go through puberty overnight and those who do not begin the transformation until their late teens. Furthermore the very label assigned to them at birth may prove to be problematic and may cause psychological discomfort in the individual; this discomfort is referred to as gender dysphoria and is described in more detail below. The biosocial approach to gender development continues to have adherents; however, Money's credibility was severely affected when the truth regarding the Joan/John case, on which he rested much of his theorising, was revealed (the case is described below). Furthermore the biosocial theory fails to expand on precisely how the social influences have an impact upon gender development.

Thinking scientifically → **The case of Joan/John**

In 1965 a pair of twin boys were born to the Reimer family in America; both boys were healthy to begin with, but at the age of six months both began to experience problems urinating. This was caused by a problem with the foreskin and so a circumcision was recommended. Unfortunately there was a mistake with one of the surgeries and one of the boys, Bruce, received extensive injuries to his penis. This damage was so severe that his penis was irreparable and the Reimers were advised to raise Bruce as a girl with appropriate hormonal and surgical treatment to complete his transformation into a female. The transformation was overseen by Dr John Money who had argued that gender is a product of nurture, rather than nature. He advised that Bruce should be raised as a girl, dressed in female clothing only and socialised to behave in feminine ways. When Bruce was 17 months old he experienced the first surgical intervention and underwent an orchiectomy (removal of the testes) and the remaining scrotal flesh was shaped to resemble labia. After this operation Bruce returned home and from that moment was treated as a girl and called Brenda.

While his family adapted to the change it became evident within a few years that the transformation was not complete as it was reported later that Brenda was something of a tomboy and had many difficulties making friends. However, John Money and his colleagues were pleased with the progress and published widely on the case arguing that this was a resounding success for nurture over nature. In these reports Bruce/Brenda was referred to as John/Joan which has remained a common name for the case. As part of Brenda's on-going treatment she and her twin brother were taken to yearly appointments at John Hopkins University where Money and colleagues carried out a battery of physical and psychological tests. As Brenda was mid-way through the gender transformation Money also invited male-to-female trans-sexuals to discuss the benefits of being female and the clinic visits were also reported to include distressing examinations of Brenda's genitals (Diamond & Sigmundson, 1997). These attempts by the medical community to force Brenda to accept her female identity came to an end when she was 14. At this time she was under increasing pressure to allow Money to perform the final operation which would manufacture a vagina, but Brenda was increasingly unhappy and resisted these efforts and determined to return to her original male identity.

At the age of 14 Brenda returned to his status as a male and renamed himself David. In the late 1990s there was a resurgence of interest in the case following an article in Rolling Stone magazine which was based on interviews with David and his family (Colapinto, 1997), and in 2000 David waived his right to anonymity. He underwent several surgeries to return his anatomy to that of a man, which included the reconstruction of a functioning penis and he went on to marry. Unfortunately David's twin brother committed suicide in 2002, and whilst still mourning David lost his job and separated from his wife. He committed suicide in 2004 at the age of 38.

The case of John/Joan is a subject of much deliberation within academic circles as it raises many questions regarding the on-going debate over the influence of nature/nurture and the implications of medical interventions in such cases. There are also suggestions that the case should be used as a warning to avoid the 'either/or' approach that medical sciences takes towards gender (Hausman, 2000).

Gender dysphoria and Gender Identity Disorder

In this section we shall explore the conditions of gender dysphoria and **Gender Identity Disorder** (GID) with a particular focus on a biosocial explanation of the experiences.

Gender dysphoria

Gender dysphoria is defined as the "persistent discomfort about one's biological sex or the sense that the gender role of that sex is inappropriate" (Butcher et al., 2008, p. 360). This is often accompanied by the desire of an individual to be the opposite sex to which they were born with, that is a male by birth would desire to become a woman and vice versa. This sense of discomfort, while often severe enough to warrant a diagnosis of GID (see below), often only lasts during childhood with the vast majority of research showing that this is most often a transitory stage during adolescence with most individuals not experiencing gender dysphoria post puberty (Drummond et al., 2008; Steensma et al., 2011). The following quote from an interview study with adolescents who had experienced gender dysphoria during childhood gives some insight into what the discomfort feels like:

> In childhood (and still), I had the feeling that I was born as a boy. I did not 'want' to be a girl. To myself I 'was' a boy, I felt insulted if people treated me as a girl. Of course I 'knew' I was a girl, but still, in my view I was not.
>
> (Steensma et al., 2011, p. 6)

In and of itself however gender dysphoria is not a psychiatric condition, but a label applied to a sense of sadness or anxiety regarding one's biological sex; in some instances this gender dysphoria may be severe enough to warrant a diagnosis of GID.

Gender Identity Disorder

Gender Identity Disorder (GID) is a psychiatric condition which features in the DSM-IV-TR, which is the current diagnostic manual of the American Psychiatric Association (2000). In order for a diagnosis to be received during childhood, four of the following must be present (ibid.):

- Repeated insistence or desire to be of the opposite sex
- The adoption of cross-gender clothing (i.e. girls wearing boys clothes and vice versa)
- Engaging in pretend or fantasy play where an opposite gender role is assumed (e.g. boys pretending to be a mother)

- Playing with toys or playing games which stereotypically belong to the opposite gender
- Preference for friends and playmates of the opposite sex.

These four must also be accompanied by a continual uneasiness and discomfort that the child has with his/her sex (i.e. gender dysphoria). A diagnosis of GID has been found to occur predominantly in boys; this is in large part due to the social acceptance of gender identity confusion in females. It is considered more socially acceptable for a girl to be a 'tomboy' and to associate with male peers, whereas it is less socially acceptable of boys to show signs of femininity (Cohen-Kettenis et al., 2003).

There have been several studies that have found that those children who receive a diagnosis of GID are more likely to be homosexual when they are adults (e.g. Drummond et al., 2008; Green, 1987; Zucker, 2005). In a recent follow-up study 25 girls who were diagnosed with GID at a mean age of 8 years were then assessed at an average age of 23 years (Drummond et al., 2008). It was found that of the 25 participants just three still met the criteria for GID; also of interest were the results regarding sexual orientation. Eight of the 25 participants were classified as homosexual in fantasy, six in activity and the rest of the participants were classified as either heterosexual or asexual. These findings are significantly higher than the base rate of homosexuality in the general population and indicate that "girlhood cross-gender identification is associated with a relatively high rate of bisexual/homosexual sexual orientation in adolescence and adulthood" (Drummond et al., 2008, p. 42).

The treatment of GID in childhood and adolescence can take several courses. Zucker and Cohen-Kettenis (2008) list five possible treatment pathways:

1 Behaviour therapy which involves the rewarding of gender-typical behaviours; this is reinforced by the non-rewarding of cross-gender behaviours.
2 Psychotherapy, including psychoanalysis, to try and explore the cause of the gender dysphoria.
3 Treatment of parents to assess their influence on the development of GID and to assist in the daily management of the condition.
4 The setting of limits on cross-gender behaviour and the encouragement of alternative activities.

5   Supportive treatments which acknowledge that the cause of GID might be biological in basis and so focus on supporting the child in their everyday environment.

Note that surgical or hormonal intervention is not listed above and is generally refrained from during childhood, predominantly because most cases of GID do not last into adulthood; therefore behavioural treatments are preferred.

There has been much advancement in recent years in attitudes towards individuals with gender dysphoria, including transsexuals. In 2004 the Gender Recognition Act was passed in the United Kingdom which recognises the right of transsexuals to have their new gender legally recognised, for example this may mean the reissuing of birth certificates to show their new gender. Despite some progress in attitudes towards transsexualism individuals are still likely to encounter some opposition and negative attitudes. While awareness of the condition is increasing gender dysphoria still remains a relatively rare condition, for example there is a reported rate of 8 per 100,000 of the population in Scotland (Wilson et al., 1999).

Biosocial approach to gender dysphoria and gender identity disorder

For some researchers, gender dysphoria/GID has a biological origin. For example, it has been found that there are sex differences in a particular area in the brain associated with sexual behaviour. There is evidence that women have a smaller part of the hypothalamus called the bed nucleus of the stria terminalis (or BSTc). In a study that looked at the BSTc of male to female transsexuals it was found that the sizes of the BSTc were closer to that of females than of males (Zhou et al., 1995). They suggest that this supports the argument that "gender identity develops as a result of an interaction between the developing brain and sex hormones" (ibid., p. 68). There has also been a suggestion (Green, 2000) that gender dysphoria/GID may run in families; whether this means a genetic basis or is due to a shared social environment remains a question for further research however.

The cause of gender dysphoria/GID remains unclear however, and it is still debated whether its origins are strictly biological. Some researchers have suggested that dysphoria/GID is a result of a combination of social and biological influences, hence favouring a biosocial approach. A recent qualitative study looked at individuals whose feelings of gender dysphoria during childhood persisted or desisted in adolescence (Steensma et al., 2011). They found that the following factors were associated with a persistence and intensification of gender dysphoria during puberty: perceived alterations in the social surroundings, expectation of physical changes and first experiences of love. Thus, we can see how both physical and social factors, as proposed by the biosocial theory, have an influence upon the experience of gender dysphoria. For those children whose dysphoria feelings ceased during adolescence it was often their first romantic relationships that had a significant impact, an increasing interest in same-gender friendships and activities (such as the wearing of make-up for girls) and the physical development of their bodies:

> Before puberty, I disliked the thought of getting breasts. I did not want them to grow. But when they actually started to grow, I was glad they did. I really loved looking like a girl, so I was glad my body became more feminine.
>
> (Steensma et al., 2011, p. 12)

Thus the changes to the body during puberty can both exacerbate and ease the gender dysphoria. The emotional, psychological and social changes that occur during puberty should also not be overlooked. The change from primary to secondary school, first encounters with romantic and sexual relationships, the increasing importance of peer relationship and a growing sense of independence can all have a significant impact upon the progression of gender dysphoria/GID. Culture is also undoubtedly an important factor interacting with biology.

◉ Culture and biology

In her seminal essay 'Throwing like a girl' (1980) Iris Marion Young discusses the way in which women in "contemporary advanced industrial, urban, and commercial society" (p. 140) have been socialised into carrying, using and experiencing their bodies in certain ways. She describes the following differences between male and female comportment:

> Typically, the masculine stride is longer proportional to a man's body than is the feminine stride to a woman's. The man typically swings his arms in a more open and loose fashion than does a woman and typically has more up and down rhythm in his step. Though we now

wear pants more than we used to, and consequently do not have to restrict our sitting postures because of dress, women still tend to sit with their legs relatively close together and their arms across their body. When standing or leaning, men tend to keep their feet further apart than do woman, and we also tend more to keep our hands and arms touching or shielding our bodies. A final indicative difference is the way each carries books or parcels; girls and women most often carry books embraced to their chests, while boys and men swing them along their sides.

(Young, 1980, p. 142)

These are differences which can be noticed everywhere and in most social situations: in bars, in the office and in the home. These differences have been accounted for in terms of a mysterious 'feminine essence' in the past, but Young argues that these are due to very real differences in which men and women experience their body.

Young (1980) argues that the majority of women interact with their bodies in a different way to men, primarily by being disconnected from the entirety of our corporeal being. So when women throw a ball, pick up a box, or in fact engage in any physical activity, women generally only engage the immediate muscles and body parts associated with that task. When women throw a ball, for example, only the arm is used in the effort, whereas men use their arm, shoulder, back, hips and thighs in the effort. Women also approach physical tasks with a different mental attitude to men which in turn affects performance. This means that women can be apprehensive, timid and cautious when attempting physical tasks (such as lifting or hiking) and are therefore unlikely to utilise the full body strength and ability available. Thus in our daily lives Young (ibid.) argues that women are likely to consider our bodies as limiting, as fragile and as an encumbrance. Thus the biological and the physical are given significance through our particular social understanding of what it means to have a female body. Our notions of being male and female are determined by cultural conventions which will be demonstrated below by an examination of a 'third gender' which exists in Samoan conceptualisations of sex and gender.

Samoan case of *fa'afafine*

The experience and category of *fa'afafine* in Independent Samoa can provide us with insights into how conceptualisations of gender and the body vary across cultures. While western traditions dictate that there are two genders only (male and female) the Samoans have an additional gender: that of *fa'afafine*. This term literally translates as "in the manner of a woman" (Vasey & Bartlett, 2007, p. 484). These individuals are biologically male, are attracted to straight men and often adopt feminine mannerisms. The adoption of feminine manners differs between *fa'afafine*, with some individuals perhaps adopting only one or two mannerisms (such as using make up) with other *fa'afafine* presenting themselves as fully female in public (Bartlett & Vasey, 2006). While these individuals may be labelled according to their sexual preference in western societies, *fa'afafine* are resolute that 'gays' and 'homosexuals' do not exist in Samoa (Bartlett & Vasey, 2006). Thus, while western societies have a category based on sexual preference (i.e. homosexuality) Samoan society has a category based on gender preference (*fa'afafine*).

Vasey and Bartlett have researched this notion of *fa'afafine* extensively (e.g. Bartlett & Vasey, 2006; Vasey et al., 2007) and in a 2007 research article they use it to critique the DSM diagnostic category of GID (discussed previously in this chapter). They argue that the DSM definition of GID is culturally bound, as the distress associated by the diagnosis is not in fact a result of internal feelings or cognitions but rather the distress arises from the reactions of others. In Samoa where there is a general acceptance of *fa'afafine* such individuals are accepted as they are into the community and so little distress arises. In western societies however where identification with the opposite gender is not as socially acceptable distress arises from the failure to meet society's expectations of gender identity. The authors argue that GID should "not occur in its current form in future editions of the DSM, because there is no sound evidence that cross-gender behaviors or identities, per se, cause distress" (Vasey & Bartlett, 2007, p. 489). Thus they conclude that it is society's reaction to those with gender dysphoria that is the cause of psychological distress and a more accepting social reaction would minimise the suffering of individuals who experience such feelings.

Chapter summary

In this chapter we have focused on the biological aspects of sex and how we physically develop into our adult male and female forms. When embryos form in the womb at first they appear asexual and slowly develop male and female organs and it is only during puberty that we finally acquire all of the features that we associate with the sexes, such as facial hair on men and breasts on women. For the majority of us this happens along a normative developmental path but for others, such as hermaphrodites and those with Turner's Syndrome, the binary of male/female can be found to be limiting. There are also psychiatric conditions, such as gender dysphoria or GID, which mean that the biology and the psychology do not always match up and connect for the individual. Thus although our contemporary British society only considers the male and female sex, in this chapter we have explored how this is something of a narrow definition. We ended this chapter with a brief exploration of how culture and biology become intertwined. The work of Young (1980) illustrates for us how we come to know our bodies in terms of cultural conceptualisations of genders; males and females sit in different ways, for example. Thus although we have the biological basis of sex we only become gendered bodies through our culture.

◉ Further reading

Fausto-Sterling, A. (2000). The sex/gender perplex. *Studies in History and Philosophy of Biological and Biomedical Sciences, 31*(4), 637–646.
Vasey, P. L. & Bartlett, N. H. (2007). What can the Samoan "fa'afafine" teach us about the Western concept of gender identity disorder in childhood? *Perspectives in Biology and Medicine, 50*(4), 481–490.
Young, I. M. (1980). Throwing like a girl: A phenomenology of feminine body comportment motility and spatiality. *Human Studies, 3*(1), 137–156.

◉ Key search terms

Adolescence
Biosocial approach to gender
Gender dysphoria
Gender Identity Disorder
Hermaphroditism
Oestrogen
Progesterone
Puberty

Sex/gender binary
Sexual dimorphism
Testosterone
Transgenderism
Transsexualism
Turner's Syndrome

Chapter 3

Gender and early childhood

In Chapters 3–5 we will take something of a chronological approach to the development of gender across childhood; Chapter 4 will look at late childhood and the school years (ages 4–11) and Chapter 5 will look at gender during adolescence. In this chapter however we will be looking at the preschool years; this is the time when gender begins to emerge and by the age of four children are aware of what gender categories are, what are gender-appropriate behaviours and what makes them a girl or a boy. Gender awareness is very basic initially, but this provides a solid foundation for the later development of more complex gender notions. This chapter will cover the following:

- Prenatal environment gender, including the physical environment and the sex preferences of parents
- Adult interactions with children of different genders
- Infants' understanding of gender
- Gender and play: the early years

Prenatal development of gender

In the previous chapter we discussed how the development of the foetus results in biological differences between newborn girls and boys. However, gender is a much bigger issue than biology, and the assignment of gender, rather than sex, begins outside of the womb as well. Think of your own encounters with expectant parents who have decided to find out the sex of their unborn baby – perhaps they have decided to paint the nursery pink upon hearing it was a girl or decorate it with a cowboy or dinosaur theme if they are having a boy.

Physical environment

It has been found that there are significant differences regarding the decoration of infants' bedrooms which act to further reinforce gender differences and stereotypes (Pomerleau et al., 1990). It has been found that boys' bedrooms are more likely to have animal motifs, whereas girls' are more likely to have floral decoration (Rheingold & Cook, 1975). Textiles are also likely to reflect gender stereotypes, with boys more likely to have blue bedding and curtains (Pomerleau et al., 1990). Thus, unsurprisingly, parents are likely to decorate their infants' bedrooms in ways that reflect stereotypical ideas of gender.

Parents are also more likely to dress their infants according to gender. In the aforementioned study by Pomerleau et al. (1990) they found that parents are more likely to give their infants pink or blue pacifiers based on gender, that female babies are more likely to wear pink and that boys are more likely to wear blue. Another study (Shakin et al., 1985) observed infants at a shopping mall in Long Island, New York, and looked at their dress and accessories (such as blankets or pacifiers); the researchers also asked the parent accompanying the child a series of questions regarding clothing choice for their children. Based on external appearances the observers were able to correctly ascertain the sex of the infant; 75 per cent of the female infants had pink clothing or accessories and 79 per cent of the boys were wearing or carrying blue. Boys were also more likely to wear red and girls more likely to wear yellow. Thus it would seem that in infants (when it is difficult to assign gender according to other features, such as hairstyle or facial structure) clothing is used as an indicator of gender.

In essence, even before the child is born we create a basic gender identity for the child according to the toys and clothing we buy and according to the decoration scheme chosen for the nursery; thus while the sex of the child is developing within the womb, the gender of the child is also developing outside of the womb.

Sex preferences of parents

When planning children, either in the short- or long-term, prospective parents often form ideas of what it will be like to have children. They might imagine what it will be like to have a newborn in the house or the child's first day at school or what family holidays will be like. They might even form an idea of what sex child they would prefer. It is a well-known problem that in some countries, such as India and China, it is more commonplace to prefer sons than daughters. This is due to a cultural preference of males over females in society and the traditional dowry costs associated with the marriage of a daughter. Hank (2007) lists China, India, Korea and Vietnam as showing a clear demographic trend for son preference, with some countries also displaying regional variation; in India, for example, the northern states demonstrate a higher level of preference for sons than the southern states (Mutharayappa et al., 1997) (the issue of son preference is explored elsewhere in the book).

However, what is not as well publicised is that similar gender preferences have also been found in western societies, with research particularly pointing to America as home to this preference for sons. The mild preference for sons has been widely reported in literature (Hank, 2007; Hoffman, 1977; Pooler, 1991) and the reasons for this preference have been stated as follows:

> It is interesting to note that the most common reasons women gave for wanting boys were to please their husbands, to carry on the family name (the husband's family name, of course), and to be a companion to the husband. The most common reasons women gave for wanting a girl were to have a companion and that it would be 'fun to dress her and fuss with her hair'. Other reasons included that the child would be more like the mother, that girls are easier to raise and more obedient, that girls could help with and learn about housework and caring for the other children, that girls stay closer to their parents than boys, and that girls are cuter, sweeter, or not as mean.
>
> (Hoffman, 1977, p. 648)

There is evidence that this preference for sons is waning as Pooler (1991) evidenced in his study of the sex preferences of college students in America. He found that over 80 per cent of male students would prefer a son, whereas female students showed a significant preference for a daughter. It must be remembered that Pooler's (1991) sample concerned a generation of women who had been raised by women involved in the second wave of feminism and who may have been experiencing the third wave of feminism for themselves. Thus it is possible that changing ideas regarding the equality of genders had an impact on this decreasing preference for sons.

Thinking scientifically → **Use of undergraduate students in psychological research**

Psychology research is dominated by the study of American college students, primarily because this is a convenient sample which researchers (i.e. lecturers) can access incredibly easily. While this sample might be appropriate for some studies, it is often a weakness in others. There are several issues of concern with the repeated use of college students as samples: firstly they are still coming to terms with their identity, may still be experiencing peer pressure and have a tendency to comply with figures of authority (Sears, 1986). There is also the criticism that for many studies that use college students this simply is not an appropriate sample, such as in the aforementioned research into sex preferences (Marleau & Saucier, 2002). This is not a recent problem though as in 1946 McNemar commented: *the existing science of human behaviour is largely the science of sophomores* (p. 333, cited in Cooper, McCord & Socha, 2011, p. 23). While the use of college students will no doubt remain the convenient sampling method of choice for some researchers, there is an increasing awareness that psychological research will be rendered invalid unless participation is widened.

However, it has been pointed out that many of the studies that looked at sex preference have used college students as a sample group (as in Pooler (1991) described above). There was a criticism that for this group the issue of sex preference was not a salient issue as they are not expectant parents and so Marleau and Saucier (2002) conducted a review which looked at the sex preference displayed by pregnant women, a sample group for whom sex preference was a relevant issue. They found that, in opposition to the research described above, mothers-to-be showed a preference for daughters, rather than sons. On the other hand fathers showed a preference for sons, as did non-expectant samples (such as college students). So there is an interesting finding here that pregnant women show a sex preference for daughters which the authors suggest might be due to the belief that girls are easier to raise or a concern with the maternal family line (Marleau & Saucier, 2002). What the results from these studies do tell us is that sex preference is strongly related to cultural events, specifically historical notions regarding gender, and while sex preferences in non-western countries (such as China and India) are relatively easy trends to understand the issue is much more complicated in the west.

Thus from an early age, in fact before their child is born, parents are beginning to socialise their children into 'being' male or female; the clothes they are dressed in and the design scheme of the nursery all create notions of gender for the infant as they develop a sense of gender and how much their parents wanted a son or daughter all begin to shape the child's gender identity.

Adult reactions to gender

As we discussed with regard to clothing earlier in the chapter adults make judgements regarding the gender of infants (Shakin et al., 1985). This is an essential part of the child learning to view itself as either male or female and so is worthy of exploration at this point. This is of particular ease to study when children are infants as their appearance is not particularly gendered; so it is easy to tell an adult male and female apart, but this is not the case during infancy when neutral clothing and baby hair mean that it can be difficult to ascertain whether the child is a baby boy or a baby girl. This was demonstrated in a study (Delk et al., 1986) in which participants were shown a videotape of a 22-month-old toddler playing and walking around; as the toddler was wearing only a diaper and a pair of neutral shoes, it was impossible for the participants to determine the sex of the infant (who was in fact female). The video was watched by 464 undergraduate students who were told that the child was male, female or a hermaphrodite. When watching the video one half of the participants had to describe the activity of the child as either masculine or feminine; the other half of the group had to describe the activity as masculine, feminine or neutral. Their results demonstrated "that adults are inclined to perceive traits in an infant that are consistent with the infant's gender label . . . in addition, it demonstrates that providing a neutral category along with masculine and feminine categories does not obviate the general trend to making sex stereotyped judgements" (Delk et al., 1986, p. 534). Furthermore, for those children labelled as hermaphrodites the masculine and feminine ratings were equal. So the gender label of the child clearly affects how their behaviours are perceived in terms of masculinity and femininity.

Adult and child play

These differences in adult responses are not just limited to observations but also have an impact upon play and interactions with the infant. A study (Frisch, 1977) looked at the differences in play behaviour between adults and infants based on the gender of the child. The study involved children aged 14–15 months and adults (12 males and 12 females) who were unknown to the infant. During the research an adult would be assigned to play with a child who had been designated either a boy or a girl for that session; thus the study was looking at the play behaviours with the perceived gender of the child, rather than the actual sex. The toddlers who were labelled as female received more verbal encouragement from the adults and were also encouraged to play in a more nurturing way (such as pretending to feed and care for a doll); on the other hand the 'male' toddlers were given more traditional male toys. The author concluded that:

> The general picture which emerges from the results of this study is one in which adults are playing in masculine ways with children whom they think are boys and in feminine ways with children whom they think are girls. The women are playing in more feminine ways overall, but the children are not showing sex differences in their own activities.
>
> (Frisch, 1977, p. 1674)

Thus it is clear that from a very early age adults are imposing gender-appropriate descriptions, activities and objects upon infants. While the attitudes of adults in general to the gender of infants are worthy of research, the approaches of parents are due further exploration as they are the primary gender models that children learn from.

Parents

The differential treatment of infants by parents begins at a very early age and was famously studied by Rubin et al. (1974). They found that parents used different adjectives to describe their newborn children; boys were more likely to be described as strong and the girls as little. They were also more likely to rate their daughters as "softer, finer featured, littler, and more inattentive than boys; the fathers were more likely than the mothers to rate the girls as softer, finer featured, more awkward, more inattentive, weaker, and more delicate than boys" (Karraker et al., 1995, pp. 687–688). Even at such an early age parents are relating to and describing their children in terms that reinforce cultural stereotypes regarding gender. However, this study was conducted in 1974 (Rubin et al.) and an updated version of the research was carried out in 1995 (Karraker et al.) to see if attitudes towards infants had changed, which was particularly important as significant steps had been taken towards gender equality in the intervening years.

The authors (Karraker et al., 1995) recruited 40 mother–father pairs (parents to 21 boys and 19 girls) to take part in their study. They were interviewed soon after their child's birth and then a week later; each parent was interviewed separately. In the interviews the parents were asked to describe their child as they would do to a close friend or relative and then to rate their infant on a number of scales; they were also asked a number of questions regarding their expectations of their child and their interactions with the baby. They found that parents described girls as weaker and more delicate than boys. However, they found fewer differences associated with gender stereotyping than the 1974 (Rubin et al.) study and concluded that there had been a weakening of these stereotyping effects. This was particularly true with regard to fathers as they found no difference in descriptions between the parents.

Another study (Smith & Lloyd, 1978) that looked at the reactions of mothers to the gender of infants used four infants who were aged six months. The infants were dressed in either male or female clothing during the experiment and the mothers were told that the study was interested in play behaviour. The mother and the infant played together for 10 minutes and there were also some toys present in the room, some of which were considered to be masculine, some feminine or neutral. Unsurprisingly the mothers offered the infants toys which matched their designated sex; furthermore the mothers actively encouraged the 'male' infants to engage in more physically vigorous play. The authors suggest that this encouragement is in keeping with the cultural notion of boys as being more physically active and adventurous. Other studies have provided evidence for the differential treatment of children by parents, based on the sex of the child (e.g. Caldera et al., 1989; Kerig et al., 1993; Leaper, 2000). So from a very early age infants are being taught that men and women are different and that, consequently, the genders behave differently.

👁 Gender and temperament

While there are many similarities between infants there are also substantial differences. Anyone who has spent time with babies knows that glimpses of character and personality start to emerge fairly soon after birth; some infants are easy to settle and rarely cry, others never seem content and cry for no apparent reason. These differences in infancy are referred to as temperament and it has been argued that there are significant gender differences in temperament. We will first look at a brief description and definition of temperament before evaluating the reported gender differences.

Temperament

There are many definitions of temperament, but in essence "temperament is frequently regarded as a constitutional predisposition, observable in preverbal infants and animals . . . Personality traits, in contrast, are often assumed to be acquired patterns of thought and behaviour that might be found only in organisms with sophisticated cognitive systems" (McCrae et al., 2000, p. 173). Thus, temperament is innate whereas personality is learned. A more detailed definition comes from Rothbart et al. (2000) who write that temperament refers to " . . . individual differences in reactivity and self-regulation assumed to have a constitutional basis" (p. 123). Reactivity refers to the levels of excitation of physiological systems, self-regulation to the modulation of this reactivity and constitutional to the biological make-up of the individual. So temperament refers to the foundations of personality that are the result of physiological biases.

In 1977 Thomas and Chess published a classic study regarding temperament. They conducted a longitudinal study which looked at the development of 138 individuals from birth to adulthood. They identified nine dimensions of temperament, which are:

- *Activity level* – This refers to the mobility level of the child.
- *Rhythmicity* – These are the patterns of a child's sleeping and feeding pattern, as well as more subtle biological processes that are cyclical.
- *Approach/withdrawal* – Refers to the interest displayed by the infant to new stimuli or environments.

- *Adaptability to new experience* – This refers to the level of difficulty (or ease) that the infant displays.
- *Threshold of responsiveness* – This is the level of stimulus required to provoke a reaction from the infant.
- *Intensity of reaction* – This refers to the level of energy within the infant's reactions.
- *Quality of mood* (positive or negative) – Generally refers to the mood displayed by the infant.
- *Persistence* – This is also known as attention span.
- *Distractibility* – This is the degree to which the infant can be distracted from its current activity.

According to Thomas and Chess (1977) the above dimensions of temperament interact to create three types of temperament. These are described in Table 3.1 as is the prevalence from the Thomas and Chess (ibid.) sample.

While temperament is described as being based on biological and physiological predispositions, there have been numerous studies that have indicated cultural differences between the temperament of infants (e.g. Gartstein et al., 2010; Montirosso et al., 2011; Super et al., 2008). In Thomas and Chess's (1977) original study, for example, part of their sample also included Puerto Rican, as well as white American, families. They found that there was a significant difference between the cultural groups in the dimension of rhythmicity which was found to have an environmental cause. It was due to the fact that no demands were made of the Puerto Rican infants in terms of a sleeping schedule; up until the age of 5 the children were allowed to sleep and wake when they wanted. This was not the case with the American parents who were keen to get their children settled into a sleeping pattern which complemented their working

TYPE	PREVALENCE	DESCRIPTION
Easy	40%	Regular and predictable cycles, positive affect and adjust to new situations easily
Difficult	10%	Irregular patterns, negative affect, irritable and resistant to change.
Slow to warm up	15%	Non-responsive and lacking in affect.

Table 3.1 Temperament types
Source: Thomas & Chess (1977).

routines. Thus there is sufficient evidence that temperament is influenced by culture. This is of particular importance when considering gender.

Gender differences in temperament

It has been found that there are slight differences in the temperament of children. In a 2006 review (Else-Quest et al.) of the literature it was reported that girls had a greater attention span and rated higher on mood (positive), shyness and approach than boys. Males however rate higher on level of activity and impulsivity. Further gender differences have been found; in 1984 (Maziade et al.) it was reported that boys were more likely to be of the extremely difficult temperament type; furthermore Gartstein and Rothbart (2003) found that males scored higher on the activity ratings. However, it is impossible to ascertain whether these findings are the result of physiological differences between the sexes or due to early effects of socialisation; the nature/nurture debate will continue with regard to this issue.

Infants' understanding of gender

One area of research that has revealed some understanding of infants' knowledge about gender has been the ability of infants to match male and female voices to appropriate photographs. Results from studies looking at this phenomenon have found that infants are able to correctly match female voices to photographs of female faces (and male voices to male faces) by approximately 9 months (Patterson & Werker, 2002; Poulin-Dubois et al., 1994). However, there has been a suggestion that this process can occur as early as 3 months (Brookes et al., 2001). Thus infants are learning very early the characteristics that are associated with the genders. Once infants have an understanding of the gender categories they can begin to apply gender labels, such as boy, girl, man and woman. It has been shown that children begin to show an understanding of gender labels by the age of 18 months (Poulin-Dubois et al., 1998) and that toddlers show a sharp increase in understanding at around 29 months (Etaugh et al., 1989).

It is not just knowledge of gender labelling that emerges in infancy, but also an awareness of gender stereotypes. A 2002 (Serbin et al.) study looked at the knowledge of 77 24-month-old children regarding gender stereotypes. The children were presented with a series of photographs which featured male and female adults engaged in identical activities; three of the images featured the adults engaged in masculine activities (such as fixing a toy), feminine activities (such as ironing) and gender-neutral activities (such as reading). The infants spent considerably more time looking at the male actor engaged in feminine activities. However, when shown photographs of the female engaged in masculine activities the children did not spend a significant amount of time looking at the images. The authors concluded that this difference in the time spent looking at the images was due to the gender division of chores that the infants witnessed at home. The parents reported that there were many chores that the mothers did (such as ironing), but that some of the traditionally masculine chores (such as fixing a toy) were also performed by women. Thus the child was exposed to many chores that they perceived as feminine, but to very few chores that were performed only by their fathers; so explaining the preferential looking displayed when the toddlers witnessed men performing tasks only performed by their mother. This demonstrates that the toddlers are already learning about gendered activities and, from the findings of this study (Serbin et al., 2002), that women are the predominant providers of labour within the household. Thus by the time children emerge from toddler-hood they have a clear understanding of gender, gender labels and gender stereotypes.

◉ Gender and play: The early years

As children grow they develop their cognitive, emotional and social skills through play, allowing them to test and expand the boundaries of their abilities. Play becomes increasingly common during the preschool years as children master control of their body and develop the ability to entertain themselves. There are significant gender differences in play which begin to emerge during the toddler years and these shall be explored in this section.

As discussed earlier children's toys are stereotyped from a very early age, even before birth as parents invest in gender-appropriate toys for their unborn babies. Thus while children may be provided with gender-appropriate toys from a very young age, they become increasingly likely to self-select gender stereotypical toys as they develop. This was demonstrated by research that observed children's play behaviour over a period of 14 months at a day-care centre in order to evaluate the effects of gender upon play (O'Brien & Huston, 1985). The participants were 52 children who ranged from 14 to 35 months, all of whom came from a middle-class background. The researchers also provided a set of gender-stereotypical toys at the day-care centre; the masculine toys included a train and truck and the female toys a doll and a tea set. Twenty-two of the children were also visited at home where the researchers were able to assess the gendered nature of their own personal toys. The children showed a clear preference for toys that were appropriate to their gender; the most popular toy among the boys was the truck and some toy tools and the girls played most often with the doll. The children also showed an increasing preference for the gender-appropriate toys as they got older, that is the older the child the more frequently they played with toys associated with their gender. The authors suggest that this developmental preference for gender-appropriate toys is associated with an increasing awareness of gender and gender roles.

A study in 1975 (Rheingold & Cook) examined the bedrooms of nearly 100 children aged between one and six. A similar study was conducted over a decade later by Pomerleau et al. (1990) which looked at how bedroom environment differed between male and female infants. The studies resulted in similar findings which were:

- More girls had dolls than boys (Pomerleau et al., 1990; Rheingold & Cook, 1975).
- Girls were, unsurprisingly, more likely to have toys for caring for their dolls, such as toy baths and bottles (Rheingold & Cook, 1975).
- If boys did have dolls, they were more likely to be male figures than female or infant dolls (Rheingold & Cook, 1975).
- Boys were more likely to have toy tools than the girls (Pomerleau et al., 1990).
- At the age of 25 months the girls were more likely to have toys regarding domestic chores (such as kitchen utensils) (Pomerleau et al., 1990).
- Boys possessed more sporting equipment and toy vehicles (Pomerleau et al., 1990; Rheingold & Cook, 1975).
- Children were likely to own toys that were associated with gendered activities; the boys, for example, were more likely to own farm toys, gas stations and medical kits, while the girls were more likely to own handbags, vacuum cleaners and doll houses (Pomerleau et al., 1990).
- Boys had more toys than girls and at age three had twice as many toys than girls (Rheingold & Cook, 1975).

It is not just toys that demonstrate the increasingly gendered identities of children, but also their choice of playmates. While the sex segregation of play is more common during the school years, it also occurs during the preschool years (Moller & Serbin, 1996). The play of preschool Canadian children has been studied in order to assess why this gender segregation occurs at such an early age, and in this study (ibid.) 57 children (28 boys and 29 girls) were observed over a 2-year period. The participant cohort was predominantly middle class, English speaking and white; the children were aged between 26 and 40 months. The child's play was measured both in terms of the toys they played with and the friends they interacted with. Overall more children played in gender-segregated groups than not; there was also a significant difference between the male and female toddlers in terms of segregation and girls were much more likely to play only with fellow females. Furthermore the girls were also more likely to play with feminine toys than masculine, and the boys were more likely to play with masculine toys. The authors (ibid.) suggest that this gender segregation is due to a difference in play behaviours, with segregated girls more likely to play in a way that demonstrates social sensitivity; in turn these girls become more likely to exclude those (such as unruly and physically more active boys) who do not fit into the prosocial nature of their activities.

◉ Chapter summary

In this chapter we have covered several areas that demonstrate how gender begins to develop in young children. Before birth parents make assumptions regarding their child's gender development and purchase suitable clothing and toys and decorate their nurseries in gender-appropriate ways. Adults also behave differently and play with infants in gender-appropriate ways, subtly and directly reinforcing social and cultural stereotypes. There are also differences between how the infants themselves behave, their temperament, while young children also learn to associate characteristics and behaviours with each of the genders. Furthermore differences in play and toy choice between the genders also become apparent, as well as early peer preferences which result in gender segregation of play. In essence children begin to develop a gender (rather than a sex) even before they are born and early on in their lives foundations are laid for later gender development.

👁 Further reading

Pomerleau, A., Bolduc, D., Malcuit, G. & Cossette, L. (1990). Pink or blue: Environmental gender stereotypes in the first two years of life. *Sex Roles*, *22*(5–6), 359–367.

👁 Key search terms

Gender and temperament
Gender and toy preference
Gender stereotypes and gender
Infants and gender
Toddlers and gender

Chapter 4

Gender and middle childhood

In this chapter we will explore the development of gender between the ages of 4 and 11: the primary school years. At this time children begin to become more active participants in their own world and extend their social environment as they enter formal education. They also develop and practice their cognitive, social and physical skills as their play becomes more sophisticated; play is, as we shall see, one of the areas where gender roles are practised and gender differences become clear. We shall also comment again on the role that the family play in gender development, particularly the influence of siblings which we have not yet discussed and the influence of the **media** upon developing gender ideals. Therefore in this chapter we will cover the following:

- Play
- Gender in the classroom, with a particular focus on teacher–student interactions and educational attainment
- Gender at home, which will look at gender and sibling relationships and the effect of the media

Play

In this section we will explore how gender is associated with play, but first it is important to establish what behaviours we are referring to when we talk about play. One of the overwhelming features of play is that it refers to behaviours that do not serve any purpose (Pellegrini & Smith, 1998); children do not engage in play to meet a goal, but do so because it is enjoyable. The most accepted definition of play comes from Krasnor and Pepler (1980) who define play as behaviours which incorporate the following four features:

- The structural aspects of the behaviours must be *flexible*.
- The child must experience a *positive affect* when engaging in the behaviour.
- There should be a *non-literality* to the behaviour; this refers to the 'pretend' aspect of play and the use of the child's imagination.
- There should be an *intrinsic motivation*, that is there is no goal to the behaviour and the child is simply playing because it is fun.

Thus play can encapsulate a range of behaviours that the child can engage in. There are many types of play behaviours and in this section we will examine four types in particular to understand how gender and play are interrelated: physical play, fantasy play, play involving technology (such as computer games) and play with toys.

Physical play

Rough and tumble play refers to physically demanding behaviours including wrestling and play fighting which begins at around 4 and is considered to be more common among boys (Pellegrini & Smith, 1998). In an observational study dating back to the early 1980s the author describes the following gender differences in rough and tumble play:

> Male sessions were more often characterised by a good deal of exuberant physical contact with one another and with the stimulus toys. The dynamics of the interaction were less likely to involve verbal structuring and were more prone to unrestrained roughhousing. Girls more often attempted to structure the session through self-generated rules and suggestions, and their play was likely to centre around novel interactions with the toys. Contact with one another tended to be verbal and not physical for the girls.
>
> (DiPietro, 1981, p. 56)

It is also suggested that rough and tumble play among boys acts to strengthen affiliations (Pellegrini, 2006) and can be a demonstration of friendship (Reed & Brown, 2000).

Generally speaking boys are much more likely than girls to list outdoor activities among their favourite pastimes (Cherney & London, 2006) and Table 4.1 gives an idea of the favourite physical activities of American children:

GENDER	ACTIVITY	PERCENTAGE
Boys	Basketball	18
	Soccer	16
	Football	13
Girls	Cycling and rollerblading	15
	Swimming	14
	Soccer	12

Table 4.1 Children's favourite sports
Source: Cherney and London (2006).

Football is of particular importance to young boys and is a way of demonstrating masculinity (Reay, 2001; Swain, 2000). Swain (2000) argues that football and the idolisation of professional footballers is of particular importance in the life of a boy as it represents many aspects of successful masculinity: the wealth, the competition, the attraction of beautiful young women and the peak of physical prowess. Thus boys adopt football as an ideal of masculine identity.

Fantasy play

Fantasy play encourages the use of the child's imagination and involves adopting characters, using objects and following storylines that are made up and created in the mind of the child. Fantasy play usually begins at the age of 2 and increases in frequency until it accounts for approximately a third of play at ages 5–6, after which age it declines (Fein, 1981). Gender differences in fantasy play have been well documented over the years with girls adopting more domestic themes in their play and reaching a more sophisticated level of storyline, character and continuance, whereas the fantasy play of boys is more physically demanding and often has a fantastic and whimsical nature to it (Pellegrini & Smith, 1998). It is often cited that boys more often indulge in fantasy play that is based on superheroes, although this viewpoint has been challenged with the argument that both boys and girls enjoy the adventure, strength and power associated with popular culture superheroes (Marsh, 2000). Furthermore it has also been reported that girls are more likely to create imaginary companions, whereas boys are more likely to adopt the persona of imagined characters (Carlson & Taylor, 2005).

In an observational study (Jones & Glenn, 1991) conducted at an English primary school researchers found the following differences between the genders with regard to pretend play:

- Girls engaged in pretend play more frequently than their male counterparts.
- When boys did engage in fantasy play they were more likely to engage in object fantasy play (where an object is imagined to be another object, so a stick may become a light sabre for example).
- Girls, on the other hand, were more likely to engage in person fantasy play, where children adopt new characters and roles (e.g. they may pretend they are a mother or a ballet dancer).
- In both boys and girls the participants were more likely to play pretending games with others, rather than play on their own.
- Children were more likely to play with same-sex friends, rather than with members of the opposite sex.
- Girls' pretend play revolved around domestic settings and everyday routine (such as household chores), whereas the boys' play was more likely to feature fictional characters and be based upon television shows.

The above points demonstrate that girls are much more likely to engage in fantasy play, but we can also see how the fantasy play serves to reinforce gender roles, particularly as the girls base their play on everyday domesticity.

Playing with technology

The development of technology in recent years has led to a whole new arena of play for a generation of children with modern consoles making home-gaming and leisure an experience a world away from the early computer games of the 1970s. Computer games are predominantly played by boys who are 1.4 times more likely than girls to play video games, to play for longer periods of time and play more often (Phillips et al., 1995); however, there is some suggestion that this gender gap between use has now closed with children aged 5–13 years playing for approximately an hour each day on the computer (Cherney & London, 2006). Boys are also more likely to choose to play video games rather than doing homework (Phillips et al., 1995).

There is also likely to be a gender difference between the games children play, with girls more likely to play games rated as feminine and boys to play masculine games (Cherney & London, 2006). However, those masculine games often offer a stereotypical portrayal of women as can be seen below:

> In one example, The Adventures of Bayou Billy (1989), the beginning of the video game shows a woman in a low-cut, red dress. This woman has large, well-rounded breasts. A man is holding her and has a knife placed at her throat. Apparently, this man has kidnapped Annabelle and Billy's mission is to save her. In another similar example, Double Dragon (1985), a woman, also depicted with large breasts and wearing a mini-skirt, is walking down the street when a man hits her, knocking her down on the sidewalk. He subsequently throws her over his shoulder and carries her away. Once again, the goal of the game is to fight your way through the stages of the game to rescue her.
>
> (Dietz, 1998, p. 435)

In a survey of video games played by children Dietz (1998) found that there were no female characters in 41 per cent of games, in 28 per cent females were portrayed only as sex objects and 21 per cent featured violence directed towards women. Thus there is a concerning representation of women in a proportion of computer games whereby they are portrayed as sexual objects, passive recipients of violence and damsels in distress in need of rescuing.

Toy play

In the previous chapter we briefly discussed how children show a preference for gender-appropriate toys from a very early age. This preference continues past toddlerhood through to childhood. In a 2006 (Cherney & London) survey of 5- to 13-year-olds children reported the following toys as their favourites (accompanied by the percentage of respondents who stated it was their favourite toy):

Gender	Toy	Percentage
Boys	Manipulative toys (such as lego and building blocks)	38
	Vehicles	18
	Action figures (such as toy soldiers)	13
Girls	Dolls	37
	Stuffed animals	17
	Educational activities (such as books)	15

Table 4.2 Children's favourite toys
Source: Cherney and London (2006).

As shown in Table 4.2 the children specified toys that were gender specific, and this was particularly true for younger girls who showed a distinct preference for feminine toys (Cherney & London, 2006).

As children become more aware of gender roles and move onto more commercial toys they are also more subject to increasing pressures concerning their body image; a study of 121 girls aged between three and six years reported that nearly half of the participants were worried they were too fat (Hayes & Tantleff-Dunn, 2010). It is not just girls who are subject to pressure regarding their body shape and size however. In a review of male action figures dating back from the 1970s researchers tracked how representations of the male body have changed in recent decades (Pope et al., 1999). They found that the figures had become much more muscular, with newer toys having distinct muscular markings on the abdomen and also become broader across the torso and shoulder area. The biceps were also considerably bigger to the point that if the figures were extrapolated to actual human size some of the figures would be larger than the biggest bodybuilders. These are similar findings to those reported regarding Barbie dolls which have a figure unattainable to most women (Brownell & Napolitano, 1995; Horton et al., 1996). Children are not only displaying gender differences and practising gendered behaviours in the way they play, but are also learning about gender through toys and, as demonstrated by the portrayal of women in video games and the body images represented by toy figures, society should be aware of the messages children are receiving.

⟨◉⟩ Gender in the classroom

Most children start school at age four or five and from this point the class-room becomes an important place for socialisation, whereas the child may only have been significantly exposed to the socialising influences of the home and childcare. At school children are introduced to a much wider range of peers and also have new adult role models to learn from. All of these new sources of learning do much to formalise gender identities that were emerging during the preschool years. An example of how impor-tant the classroom is in gender socialisation comes from Reay (2001) who reported research that had been conducted in an inner London primary school with children aged 7–8. The researcher spent one year working with one particular class (14 girls and 12 boys) during which time she collected observational, interview and focus group data. The mass of data collected revealed that even at this young age the children were aware of cultural notions which positioned girls as more mature and conscientious than boys. The boys displayed a lack of interest in schoolwork and their attention was instead focused on football; playing the game at breaks and secretly swapping football cards in the classroom. There was also a dis-course present among the boys which labelled certain girls as stupid. The gendered behaviours, or femininities, that were present in the behaviours of the female pupils were slightly more complex and were divided into four groups:

1 The 'nice girls' was a group that was predominantly comprised of the middle-class students. These girls were high-achieving and very conscientious; however they did display self-critical behaviours. These self-critical behaviours have been described elsewhere (in particular by Walkerdine et al., 2002) and this appears to be a phenomenon particularly present in middle-class females who strive for educational perfection and are extremely self-disapproving when these high standards are not met. The 'nice girls' however were often viewed negatively by their classmates who viewed them as boring and lacking 'toughness'.

2 The second social grouping of females was the 'girlies' who, while studious and educationally successful, spent a lot of their time promoting heterosexual romance in the playground. They occupied themselves by writing love letters to boys and discussing the blossoming or potential relationships.

3 The 'spice girls' were, like the 'girlies', also interested in promoting relationships with the boys, but were more active in

their chasing of boys, whereas the 'girlies' were more passive in their approach. They, for example, "described the same activity – rating the boys – as their favourite playground game. As Carly explained, 'you follow the boys around and give them a mark out of ten for how attractive they are'" (Reay, 2001, p. 160). These girls were assertive and often made attempts to display their power by objectifying and challenging the boys; unfortunately they were often viewed negatively by the boys and by the teachers.

4   The final group of girls was the 'tomboys' who sought to reject behaviours associated with femininity and adopt a masculine identity. The 'tomboys' were viewed with respect by both the boys and the girls; however, interestingly, the 'tomboys' still assigned superiority to the boys; one of them, for example, was observed on 16 different occasions asserting that boys were better than girls.

While there are these four different types of femininities in the classroom, all of them (bar the 'spice girls') positioned themselves as inferior to the boys, as the author writes:

> Peer group discourses constructed girls as harder working, more mature and more socially skilled. Yet, all the boys and a significant number of the girls, if not subscribing to the view that boys are better, adhered to the view that it is better being a boy.
>
> (Reay, 2001, p. 164)

Thus while the girls may be doing better academically than the boys, there still remains a discourse and a culture in the classroom that promotes being male as better than being female.

◉ Gender gaps in science and maths

An area of research that has attracted considerable attention from academics and policy makers is the reported gender gap in science, technology and maths (known as the STEM subjects), particularly as women are considerably under-represented in careers in these areas. There is a persistent stereotype that females are worse at maths than males, however evidence for this remains disputed with some research finding no evidence for a gender gap (Else-Quest et al., 2010; Hyde et al., 2008) and other research finding in favour of a gender gap (Penner & Paret, 2008; Robinson & Lubienski, 2011). While there are debates regarding attainment, the perception of parents, teachers and children themselves is that males are better at maths than females (Lindberg et al., 2010). What has proved crucial is the difference in the attitude of the genders towards mathematics. In a 1999 study (Spencer et al.) male and female students performed equally well on a maths assessment; however, if the female participants were told just before starting the test that there was a prevailing stereotype that females were bad at maths, then the females performed significantly worse. Consequently the mere presence of a stereotype (whether the stereotype is true or not is another matter) is enough to impact performance and so the prevailing stereotype that women are not very good at maths or science may be the cause as to why women are under-represented in these career fields (Nosek et al., 2009).

Thinking scientifically → School years

As a lot of research is conducted in the United States, the authors often report the ages of their participants in terms of school grades. This can cause some confusion if not familiar with the American schooling system. Below is a table which details the correlation between age and school year in the United Kingdom and United States:

Age	UK	America
4–5	Reception	Pre-K
5–6	Year 1	Kindergarten
6–7	Year 2	1st Grade
7–8	Year 3	2nd Grade
8–9	Year 4	3rd Grade
9–10	Year 5	4th Grade
10–11	Year 6	5th Grade
11–12	Year 7	6th Grade
12–13	Year 8	7th Grade
13–14	Year 9	8th Grade
14–15	Year 10	9th Grade or Freshman Year
15–16	Year 11	10th Grade or Sophomore Year
16–17	Year 12	11th Grade or Junior Year
17–18	Year 13	12th Grade or Senior Year

One of the biggest areas of academic research that has emerged is the difference in teacher–student interaction and this has shown to have significant correlations with gender as we shall now explore.

Teacher and student interactions

While some of the research in this section will include research done with older children, it was decided to include it here as this is the period when gender differences in teacher–student interactions emerge. Table 4.3 demonstrates some of the differences that have been found relating to gender and teacher–student interactions:

AUTHORS	YEAR	COUNTRY	FINDINGS OF THE STUDY
French & French	1984	UK	Boys were more likely to speak out in class and receive attention from the teacher. This was exacerbated by a small group of boys who spoke out a disproportional amount.
Eccles & Blumenfeld	1985	America	Of the teachers' communications just 29 per cent was directed at girls, as opposed to 39 per cent towards boys; but boys were more likely to receive more negative feedback from teachers.
Jungworth	1991	Austria	Boys are more successful during interactions with teachers and through this display more competence than girls.
Öhrn	1993	Sweden	Boys are more outspoken and demanding of teachers, whereas girls are more accepting and unquestioning of the teachers' authority.
Younger et al.	1999	UK	Teachers provided less positive support for male students.
Duffy et al.	2001	Canada	There was a tendency for teachers to direct more talk towards male students.
Dee	2007	America	Students are likely to do better with a same-sex teacher which is a significant finding given that the majority of teachers are female.

Table 4.3 Gender differences in teacher and student interaction

While Table 4.3 indicates that boys receive more attention in the classroom than girls, the story is a little more complex than that which can be seen if we look at one of the aforementioned studies in more detail. In a longitudinal study (Eccles & Blumenfeld, 1985) it was found that of the teachers' communications just 29 per cent were directed at girls, as opposed to 39 per cent towards boys (the remaining talk was directed to groups of both male and female students). However, while this at first seems like preferential treatment of the male students, the researchers analysed what the content of the communications was. The boys received more verbal information regarding procedures, whereas the talk directed at the girls concerned academic matters (of the talk about academic performance, 37 per cent of talk was directed at girls, and 22 per cent at boys); the boys also received more negative attention from teachers, even when their behaviour was similar to that of girls. Furthermore the female students were also more likely to conform to classroom rules and norms and to feel bad if they broke those expectations (Eccles & Blumenfeld, 1985). Thus there are significant differences in interactions according to gender which is the result of both student (such as females being more subservient and conscientious (Eccles & Blumenfeld, 1985; Öhrn, 1993)) and teacher behaviours (such as giving more attention to boys (Duffy et al., 2001; Eccles & Blumenfeld, 1985)). It should be remembered that the classroom is not immune to the cultural norms that operate in the wider society, but is a particular environment which is influenced by these social factors and more micro-factors such as the gender and attitude of the teachers, students and parents.

Educational attainment

Children of both genders perform much the same in their early years of schooling, although some differences have been recorded. In a study that looked at the educational attainment of children in reception class (aged 4–5 years) in England they found that maths performance was equal for both boys and girls, but that in terms of reading skills the girls significantly outperformed the boys (Tymms et al., 1997). At Key Stage 1 (age 7) in England it has been found in recent years that girls outperform boys on all four areas of testing: reading, writing, maths and science. The gap between male and female mathematics performance is the smallest with girls performing just 3 per cent better than the boys, but this gap is largest with regard to writing (11 per cent) (Department for Education, 2010a). At Key Stage 2 (age 11) girls continue to significantly outperform boys in English (with a difference of approximately 9 per cent), but boys have slightly overtaken girls in mathematics performance (by 0.5 per cent) (Department for Education, 2010b). The continuing higher performance of girls has resulted in a "growing popular and academic obsession with boys' underachievement both in the UK and abroad" (Reay, 2001, p. 154). However, there has been little agreement on the cause and solution to this phenomenon. Further differences in attainment relating to gender will be explored in the next chapter.

◁◉▷ Gender at home

Other than school, the other predominant source of gender socialisation during this period is the home and family which has been discussed in the previous chapter. Children learn how to be male or female through a gradual process which takes place over countless micro-interactions between the child and other individuals and also by the child witnessing the behaviours of others:

> Consideration of the larger system of family relationships is important, first, because children acquire information about gender roles and norms via their exposure to other dyadic relationships in the family. For example, children may observe sex-typed behaviors in their mothers' and fathers' interactions with one another or be exposed to a sex-typed division of labor in the marriage relationship. Experiences with different family members also provide a point for social comparisons: children's schemas about gender roles may be shaped by their differential experiences with their mothers versus with their fathers and by the differential treatment of sisters versus brothers in their families.
>
> (McHale et al., 2003, p. 126)

One small way in which the child learns about gendered behaviour, for example, is through speech and it has been found that mothers talk more than fathers, using more supportive dialogue, whereas fathers use more directive language (Leaper et al., 1998); thus creating the notion for children that women are more verbal and more supportive than men, whereas men are more authoritative. Similarly traditional gender stereotypes are often reinforced as the mother does the majority of the childcare and fathers are conceptualised within the household as the parent in charge of discipline (Valentine, 1997). There are also differences in parent–child play that transmit cultural notions of gendered bodies; mothers engage in less physical play than fathers for example (MacDonald & Parke, 1986). When fathers do play physically with their children, there is also a gender difference in the nature of play, sons are wrestled with, yet girls are sat on their father's knee to play pattycake (ibid.). Thus early on children are taught that males and females use their bodies differently. Furthermore children are socialised differently by parents according to gender, with daughters encouraged to use more emotional talk and engage in more detailed conversations regarding emotions (Fivush, 1989; Fivush et al., 2000; Kuebli & Fivush, 1992)

The gender role attitude of the father is also found to be particularly influential. When a father has a more traditional gender role attitude then his children (both male and female) are more likely to conform to these stereotypes, whereas if he is more open and less traditional then his children are less liable to adopt these traditional gender roles (McHale & Crouter, 2003). However there is one family relationship which we have not yet discussed: the role of siblings.

Siblings

While we have discussed the effects of parents on the development of gender, we have not yet mentioned the role of siblings. In 2010 46 per cent of families in the United Kingdom had one dependent child, 39 per cent had two and 15 per cent had three or more (ONS, 2011); thus the majority of families are home to more than one child and so the role of the sibling cannot be ignored and sibling behaviour associated with gender begins very early on in the sibling relationship. A 1990 (Blakemore) study observed interactions between sibling pairs where the older sibling had a mean age of 66 months and the younger sibling was approximately 6 months and looked at 4 possible sibling combinations: sister/sister, brother/brother, older sister/younger brother and older brother/younger sister. The observations took place at the family home and over the course of four months the researcher collected data regarding the everyday interactions and behaviours witnessed between the siblings. It was found that older sisters interacted much more frequently with their infant sibling (whether a brother or sister) than the older brothers did, whether playing with it, talking to it or being involved in baby care. Thus girls were already displaying more nurturant behaviours than boys and also establishing a maternal aspect to their sibling relationship.

Another study (Stoneman et al., 1986) which again observed pairs of siblings at their home found that sister/sister dyads were less likely to play competitively and that those pairings with an older sister were more likely to play house and play with dolls. Older brother/younger sister pairs were more likely to engage in art and brother/brother pairs were the most likely to play with toys. There was also a general gender divide between activities with those siblings (male/male and older male/younger female), with an older brother taking part in more traditional male play pursuits (such as playing with toy guns, cars and trucks). Likewise, those with older sisters (sister/brother and sister/sister) were more liable to engage in stereotypically female play (such as playing with dolls and playing dress up). With regard to interactive behaviours the older sisters were much more likely than the older brothers to manage and teach their younger siblings and engage in more positive touch, while younger sisters were more likely to take on the role of learner if they had an older sister. The gender of the older sibling has a significant impact on the gendered nature of the dyads play behaviours: "for example, little boys with older brothers never played with dolls or played house, while boys with older sisters engaged in these female activities as frequently as the pairs containing two girls" (Stoneman et al., 1986, p. 507). Furthermore sister/sister and older sister/younger brother dyads are likely to be closer and have a more intimate relationship than older brother/younger sister pairs (Dunn et al., 1994) and are likely to rate their relationship quality as significantly higher if they are of the same sex (Furman & Buhrmester, 1985).

The sex of the children influences not only the siblings' relationship, but also the relationships between parents and children. It has also been found that children with opposite sex siblings are more likely to 'pair off' with the same-sex parent and that gendered activities are intensified when there are different-sex siblings (Crouter et al., 1995).

> In our sample, firstborn siblings are, on average, about 3 years older than their sisters or brothers, and it is typical for older siblings to spend more time on chores relative to younger ones. The effects of the sibling sex constellation are evident, however, when we examine families with mixed-sex sibling dyads: the discrepancy between siblings' time in household tasks is greatest for older sisters with younger brothers, and older brother/younger sister pairs are the only dyads in which the younger sibling is more involved in housework than the older one.
>
> (McHale & Crouter, 2003, p. 209)

Thus there still seems to be a traditional gender split in household chores, where girls are expected to help out more around the house, even if they have an older brother. Similarly younger sisters are involved in more household chores than younger brothers (McHale & Crouter, 2003). Consequently from an early age children absorb information regarding gender appropriate behaviours and roles from those close to them.

The media

At this point it is worth drawing attention to a particular phenomenon within our contemporary culture: the media. In recent years there has been something of a media explosion; there are now hundreds of television channels and the internet has impacted upon our daily lives in ways that were unimaginable a decade or two ago. Our social, professional and leisure lives are now intricately entwined with media and technological inventions that have literally changed our lives.

To understand why media is of importance when studying gender it is important to understand just how prevalent the media is within our daily lives; it has been said that "by the time today's children reach age 70, they will have spent 7 to 10 years of their lives watching only television" (Strasburger, 1989, cited in Strasburger, 2004, p. 55). Increases in technology mean that this level of interaction is only set to increase as it is now possible with the latest mobile communications technology to keep in touch with the latest television programmes and news anywhere and at any time. This means that children are now subject to a near limitless expanse of influence that their parents may have little control over. It is almost impossible for parents to monitor every television programme or website that their children may come into contact with, particularly given the developments in mobile communications.

This media influence includes the portrayal of gendered behaviours and gender roles which can work to inform children of what it means to 'be' male or female. In a 1993 (Furnham and Bitar) study, for example, a content analysis of television adverts was carried out and the following results reported:

- Males were more likely to do voiceovers.
- Females were more likely to be seen as the users of products.
- Men were more frequently portrayed as experts.

- Females were more frequently portrayed in the home.
- There were more young females.
- There were more older males.
- There was most frequently a male voice for end comment.

Thus we can see how men were generally constructed as the 'expert' while women were portrayed in a more domesticated role. This is in keeping with cultural stereotypes and it is interesting that this was a study conducted with adverts as this is a message that could be replayed several times during a viewing period.

The media have also come under fire from gender researchers for providing children with a false impression of what it is to 'be' male or female. In a 2003 (Martínez-González et al.) study of nearly 3000 female teenagers it was reported that the chance of an eating disorder doubled with regular reading of magazines aimed at young women. Similar findings were reported when a study (Borzekowski et al., 2000) found that the more 14- to 15-year-olds watched music videos the more dissatisfied these young women were with their body shape. The argument made by many researchers and commentators is that young women are receiving from the media a false notion of the female body and are likely to compare themselves with unattainable ideals. Famous research looking at 'Playboy' centrefolds have found that the women are more likely to be portrayed as having larger breasts, but less fat than in previous years (Garner et al., 1980; Wiseman et al., 1992). However, it is not just young women who are subject to changing physical ideals, but also men. In recent years it has been found that 'Playgirl' centrefolds are becoming increasingly muscular and also have a decreasing level of fat. In a related study (Pope et al., 1999) it was found that the changing body shapes of male action toys had also altered over the years; GI Joe had an increasing level of muscular definition and the characters of Luke Skywalker and Hans Solo had developed the frame of a bodybuilder which was a notable change from the original figures from the 1970s.

The media must be considered in any contemporary understanding of gender as it exerts such a ubiquitous influence; it is literally impossible to escape the media in contemporary western society. It is therefore of great importance to consider the messages that the media are sending to developing children regarding gender and what effects this has upon the development of their gender identity.

◉ Chapter summary

In this chapter we have explored some of the areas of influence that shape the continuing gender identity development of children. We looked at three areas in particular: play, school and the family. We clarified what the definition of play is and then looked at how types of play and certain toys are affected by and contribute to gender identities. We then looked at school which is a predominant developmental change during this period as children enter the formal education system and enter the world of school work, exams and teachers. We examined how teacher–student interactions are subject to gender differences and also looked at differences between male and female students with regard to gender. Finally we looked at the role of the family and of siblings in particular. To summarise, during this period children are subject to an increasingly wide range of influence which continues to contribute to and build upon the foundations of the gender knowledge that was established in the preschool years.

◉ Further reading

Beaman, R., Wheldall, K. & Kemp, C. (2006). Differential teacher attention to boys and girls in the classroom. *Educational Review, 58*(3), 339–366.

Cherney, I. D. & London, K. (2006). Gender-linked differences in the toys, television shows, computer games, and outdoor activities of 5- to 13-year-old children. *Sex Roles, 54*(9/10), 717–726.

McHale, S. M. & Crouter, A. C. (2003). How do children exert an impact on family life? In A. C. Crouter & A. Booth (Eds.) *Children's influence on family dynamics: The neglected side of family relationships* (pp. 207–220). Mahwah, New Jersey: Lawrence Erlbaum Associates.

◉ Key search terms

Gender and classroom
Gender and family
Gender and play
Gender and teacher
Gender gap in mathematics
Rough and tumble play

Chapter 5

Gender and adolescence

In this chapter we will explore the experiences of young men and women as they come to terms with their gender development through adolescence; in essence we will be looking at the years of 11–18. This is a period of great change in an individual's life as they progress from having a child's body to being considered an adult, both legally and physically, by the age of 18 in the United Kingdom. Adolescents have to contend with greater educational demands as they are forced to consider their future career development, come to terms with their sexuality, address changes in their personal relationships and find their adult identity. We will explore the following points which might have an impact upon the gender development and identity of an adolescent:

- Peer relationships, including bullying
- Sexuality, including gender differences in sexual behaviours and the impact of teenage pregnancy
- Education

👁 Peer relationships in adolescence

Adolescence is a significant period in terms of friendship as children move schools, meet new people and make friendships that may last a lifetime. The opportunity to engage with a variety of people also increases as adolescents extend their social network outside of school and make the move towards independence and adulthood. There are significant gender differences that have been reported with regard to friendships, for example girls are more likely to name a best friend and belong to a clique than boys are (Urberg et al., 1995). It has also been found, for example, that girls are more likely to develop closeness in a friendship through talking and the disclosure of secrets, whereas boys are more likely to become close through shared activities (McNelles & Connolly, 1999). The average friendship group size for both boys and girls is five to eight and girls are more likely to have social networks that are embedded within school, whereas boys experience more diversity in their friendship groups (Urberg et al., 1995). As adolescents age they are also more likely to form friendships outside of school and with more members of the opposite sex, this is particularly true for females who are more likely to form friendships with people older than them (Poulin & Pederson, 2007). While friendships can be a form of great support and joy during adolescence, peers can also cause considerable distress, particularly in the case of bullying.

Gender and bullying

This section has been included here, rather than in the previous chapter, as it has been shown that bullying peaks when children make the progression between schools (Pellegrini & Long, 2002) which in the case of the United Kingdom would be the transition between primary and secondary school. So what is bullying? The English term 'bullying' can be "characterized by the following three criteria: (1) it is aggressive behaviour or intentional 'harmdoing' (2) which is carried out repeatedly and over time (3) in an interpersonal relationship characterized by an imbalance of power" (Olweus, 1999, pp. 10–11, cited in Smith et al., 2002, p. 1120). Thus a one-off fight or an on-going feud between two equally matched children would not be classed as bullying according to this definition: there has to be an imbalance of power (whether according to age or size), the intent to harm has to be present and it has to occur over a period of time. This is the English language definition though, and it should be recognised that there are different terms to describe bullying-type behaviours in different cultures and languages. In Norwegian, for example, there is *mobbning* which refers to group aggression against an individual and which begins and subsides very rapidly, whereas the Japanese term *ijima* refers less to the physical aggression, but more to the social manipulation and subtle verbal aggression (Smith et al., 2002); thus each culture has its own specificities regarding the language and nature of bullying behaviours.

Statistics regarding the prevalence of bullying vary according to age and the country the research has been conducted in, but here are some indications as to how common bullying behaviours are in school:

- In the United Kingdom, roughly 75 per cent of children aged between 11 and 16 stated they had been the victim of bullying within the previous school year (Glover et al., 2000).
- 29 per cent of 11- to 12-year-olds in California reported being a victim (9 per cent), a bully (7 per cent) or both (6 per cent) (Juvonen et al., 2003).
- In the United Kingdom 42 per cent of 11- to 12-year-olds reported being the victim of verbal bullying, which increased to 55 per cent of 12- to 13-year-olds, 47 per cent of 13- to 14-year-olds, 46 per cent of 14- to 15-year-olds and fell to 35 per cent of 15- to 16-year-olds (Glover et al., 2000).
- In a study of 5171 Norwegian students aged between 11 and 15 years, 3379 reported that they had never been bullied, 1061 reported they had been bullied only once or twice, 211 reported they were bullied two or three times a month and 274 reported that they were bullied once a week or more (Solberg & Olweus, 2003).
- Research in Korean schools with adolescents aged 13–16 years revealed that 14 per cent of students reported themselves as victims, 17 per cent as perpetrators and 9 per cent as both victim and perpetrator (Kim, Koh & Leventhal, 2004).
- Australian research reported that, of 3918 students aged 11–16, 23.7 per cent bullied other students, 12.7 per cent were bullied and 21.5 per cent were both bullies and victims (Forero et al., 1999).

As can be witnessed above, there is some variation in levels of bullying according to age and country, however the statistics demonstrate that bullying is a significant aspect of life for many children.

It has been consistently shown that boys are more likely to engage in overt forms of bullying behaviour, with reported prevalence rates of 5 per cent for girls and 9 per cent for boys (Olweus, 1991). However, there are important differences between genders in the nature of bullying; boys are more likely to engage in overtly aggressive and physical bullying, whereas girls participate in more subtle, manipulative and verbal forms of bullying (Smith & Gross, 2006). In a focus group study (Owens et al., 2000) with fifty-four 15-year-old Australian females it was demonstrated that rather than the physically aggressive bullying behaviours shown by boys, females tend to display more subtle forms of aggression. The girls were found to talk about each other behind each other's back (referred to as 'bitching'), reveal secrets, spread rumours, make negative comments regarding appearance or character, ostracise the victim from the peer group, engage in verbal harassment and non–physical harassment (such as staring at the victim). The most common reason given for engaging in these behaviours "was just simply 'for something to do' – it is something to say, some conversation to overcome boredom in their daily lives. In addition, the rumor creates excitement, as girls are eager to find out the 'goss'" (Owens et al., 2000, p. 78). The behaviours were also found to relate to peer processes, such as establishing group membership (Owens et al., 2000).

◉ Sexuality and relationships

While adolescence is a significant period for friendship, it is also a significant period for romantic relationships as it is during adolescence that teenagers are likely to experience love, heartbreak and sex for the first time. Surprisingly it is an area that has received little academic interest until recently (Collins, 2003). This is a shame as it has been reported that 25 per cent of 12-year-olds, approximately 50 per cent of 15-year-olds and 70 per cent of 18-year-olds have reported being in a romantic relationship and that a significant proportion of these relationships have lasted for 11 months or longer (Carver et al., 2003); thus romantic relationships are of great importance during adolescence. Those adolescents with large networks of friends, consisting of both male and female friends, are more likely to participate in romantic relationships earlier (Connolly & Johnson, 1996; Fering, 1999). It has also been shown that success in romantic relationships is also closely related to success in peer relations (Fering, 1999; Neemann et al., 1995).

Thinking scientifically → **The age of consent**

One reason that researchers must be ethically sensitive when investigating sexual behaviour in adolescents is that it may mean participants disclosing that they have engaged in sexual activity before the age of consent. The following list provides an idea of how the heterosexual age of consent compares around the world:

China – 14 years
France – 15 years
Ghana – 16 years
Jamaica – 16 years
New Zealand – 16 years
Nigeria – 13 years
United Kingdom – 16 years
USA, Missouri – 17 years
USA, Rhode Island – 16 years
Vietnam – 18 years

There are also several countries (such as Iran, Oman and Saudi Arabia) where there is no age of consent, just the proviso that the couple is married. There are also several countries where homosexual sex (both male/male and female/female) remains illegal, such as Tunisia, Nigeria and Mauritius.

Adolescence is also a significant period for gay, lesbian and bisexual teenagers and the average age of disclosure (or 'coming out') to parents is now 16, down from age 20 a decade ago (Harrison, 2003). During the process of disclosure, the adolescent usually tells a sibling first, usually a sister, then the mother, and then the father with disclosure aided by strong support networks, the expectation of a positive reaction and a high level of self-esteem and resiliency (ibid.). A 1992 (Remafedi et al.) study surveyed nearly 35,000 American high school students and found that 88.2 per cent classed themselves as heterosexual, 1.1 per cent defined themselves as bisexual or homosexual and 10.7 per cent were unsure as to their sexuality. It was also reported that 4.5 per cent experienced same-sex attractions, 2.6 per cent reported homosexual fantasies and 1 per cent reported sexual experiences with the same sex (ibid.). Thus even if the percentage of teenagers who disclose themselves to be homosexual is relatively low the number of adolescents who report confusion regarding their sexuality is significantly higher. It is also important as homosexual adolescents are more likely to experience a higher level of bullying (DuRant et al., 1998; Warwick et al., 2001), more drug use (DuRant et al., 1998), more frequent suicidal tendencies (Kourany, 1987; Lebson, 2002; Remafedi et al., 1998) and higher levels of mental health problems (Remafedi, 1987; Ryan et al., 2009).

Teenagers and sex

The average age for first sexual intercourse is approximately 16, for both males and females (Tripp & Viner, 2005). Overall it has been suggested that by the age of fourteen 13–35 per cent of American adolescents have engaged in sexual intercourse, rising to 50–70 per cent by the ages of 16–17 and 70–90 per cent by the age of 18 (Zimmer-Gembeck & Helfand, 2008). There is also some variation between ethnicities, with black males nearly three times more likely to engage in intercourse than white adolescents (ibid.). It has also been found that although fewer girls are sexually active, those who are engage in as much sexual activity as their male peers (De Gaston & Weed, 1996). In a review (Zimmer-Gembeck & Helfand, 2008) of longitudinal studies regarding adolescent sexual behaviour the following factors have been identified in adolescents engaging in intercourse at an earlier age: early physical maturation, higher levels of alcohol consumption, lower educational aspirations and peers who have permissive attitudes towards sex. It has been argued that religious participation also significantly affects the sexual attitudes of teenagers (Werner-Wilson, 1998). It was also found that those adolescents who waited until later (18 years or older) were more likely to come from families that contained both biological parents (Zimmer-Gembeck & Helfand, 2008).

Given the media and social policy focus on teenage motherhood, adolescent use of contraception has been the focus of significant academic interest, particularly as the United Kingdom remains low in the league tables with regard to safe sex, as can be seen from the summary given in Table 5.1.

COUNTRY	STATISTICS
Netherlands	85 per cent of 'young people'
Denmark	80 per cent of 15–16-year-olds
Switzerland	80 per cent of 'adolescents'
United States	78 per cent of 'adolescents'
France	74 per cent of 'girls' and 79 per cent of 'boys'
New Zealand	75 per cent of 'sexually active teenagers'
United Kingdom	50 per cent of under 16s; 66 per cent of 16–19-year-olds

Table 5.1 Proportion of adolescents using contraception at first intercourse
Source: Tripp and Viner (2005).

So why might teenagers choose not to use contraception? The following reasons have been suggested: scepticism as to whether contraception is effective, dislike of the sensation of condoms, dislike of the long-term effects of the contraceptive pill, contraception not thought of in the heat of the moment or if too drunk and stopping using contraception when they have come to trust their partner (Skinner et al., 2009). In essence there were a variety of reasons that the teenagers gave for choosing not to use contraception. When contraception is used by teenagers, it is often used to prevent pregnancy, rather than the transmission of STIs (Sexually Transmitted Infections) (Kirkman et al., 1998). This is often because to raise the issue of the prevention of STIs could be seen to imply that the sexual partner was 'contaminated' as demonstrated in the following quote:

> Any insistence on wearing a condom could be interpreted as undermining the trust implied in the intimacy of coitus. Bonnie said that to ask a boy to wear a condom, 'if the girl was already on the pill, it might be like, yeah, accusing them of having an STD or sleeping around or something like that'. There is evidence that young people regard STDs with revulsion (Rosenthal & Moore, 1994). How can someone whom you profess to trust be accused, however obliquely, of putting you at risk of something so dirty and disgusting?
>
> (Kirkman et al., 1998, p. 359)

One of the most serious and life-changing consequences of unprotected sex is the risk of teenage pregnancy, and because this has received so much attention in academia and in the popular press this shall be explored in the next section.

Teenage pregnancy

Table 5.2 demonstrates that while the United Kingdom does have high rates of teenage pregnancy, the conception rate for young women is falling and has consistently done so in recent years.

It should be noted that Table 5.2 refers only to rates of conception and not births and so includes pregnancies that end in miscarriage and abortion. While it is often teenage motherhood that grabs the newspaper headlines, it should also be observed that an abortion or a miscarriage is a significant emotional experience in the lives of teenagers (Brady et al., 2008).

YEAR	UNDER-18 CONCEPTION RATE	UNDER-16 CONCEPTION RATE
1998	46.6	8.8
1999	44.8	8.2
2000	43.6	8.3
2001	42.5	8.0
2002	42.7	7.9
2003	42.1	7.9
2004	41.6	7.5
2005	41.3	7.8
2006	40.6	7.7
2007	41.8	8.3
2008	40.5	7.8
2009	38.2	7.5

Table 5.2 Teenage conception rates
Source: ONS & Department for Education (2011).

A 2007 (Imamura et al.) review of literature regarding teenage pregnancy reported the following risk factors associated with teenage pregnancy:

- The most reported risk factor was lower socioeconomic status.
- Those girls raised in a single-parent household are more likely to become teenage mothers.
- Disliking school and leaving school at the earliest opportunity (16 in the United Kingdom) was also highly correlated with teenage pregnancy.
- Those females engaging in sexual behaviour earlier were also more likely to become teenage mothers.

While there were other behaviours that were associated with teen pregnancy (such as smoking and binge drinking), by far the biggest three risk factors were low socioeconomic status, unstable family environment and low education (ibid.).

Teenage pregnancy is not just about the mothers, but also about the fathers. The majority of teenage pregnancies occur in relationships that do not involve co-habitation, let alone marriage, therefore the involvement of the father can differ between families. It has been found that the involvement of the grandparents has a great effect on the level of involvement of the fathers; this is unsurprising given that both teenage parents are likely to be living with their parents at the time of conception and even after the child has been born. Furthermore a father is more likely to be involved if his parents (the child's paternal grandparents) are also involved in the lives of the mother and child (Kalil et al., 2005). Teenage fathers are also more likely to come from young parents themselves, to come from low-income families and to receive a low level of education; thus the fathers are unlikely to be able to secure profitable employment which impacts upon their ability to provide for their own family (Bunting & McAuley, 2004). The outcomes for teenage fathers do not tend to be positive with an increased likelihood of financial hardship, delinquent behaviour and a decreasing level of contact with the child (Bunting & McAuley, 2004). However, despite the majority of reports finding negative outcomes, there is a minority of teenage fathers who remain dedicated parents to their children.

⊙ Education

We discussed in the previous chapter the educational differences between males and females, including early signs of girls outperforming boys in standardised testing and differences in teacher–student interactions in the classroom. For older children the educational attainment of the genders can be measured through the qualifications teenagers acquire. Table 5.3 gives a comparison of GCSE (General Certificate in Education which is sat in the United Kingdom when children are 16 years old) attainment rates between male and female students.

YEAR	FEMALE STUDENTS	MALE STUDENTS	DIFFERENCE (IN FAVOUR OF GIRLS)
2005/2006	92.5	87.8	4.7
2006/2007	93.1	88.8	4.3
2007/2008	93.6	89.6	4
2008/2009	94.4	90.4	4
2009/2010	94.4	90.8	3.6

Table 5.3 Percentages of students achieving 5+ GCSEs, grades A*–G
Source: Department for Education (2010).

As we can see there is a consistent difference between male and female scores with 4 per cent of girls consistently attaining five or more GCSEs than their male counterparts; however, the difference between male and female attainment is even more marked at the higher grade level. In 1994 in Scotland 28 per cent of girls obtained four or more GCSEs graded A–C, as opposed to 24 per cent of boys (Tinklin, 2003). It has been suggested that the peer relationships of girls are more likely to foster academic attainment, whereas male friendships in school discourage academic success and it is suggested that girls are more likely to take school seriously and thus perform better (ibid.). The results are not just limited to Scotland but are witnessed in England and Wales as can be seen in Table 5.4.

Thus while there is an approximate difference of 4 per cent between the number of students attaining 5+ GCSEs, there is a much bigger difference of approximately 9 per cent between genders when considering the higher grades only.

At A'Level (sat in the United Kingdom when teenagers are 18) there is some catch-up between the attainment levels of genders as can be seen in Table 5.5. Also noteworthy is the difference between male and female students enrolled for this higher qualification.

Traditionally it has been assumed that there is a gender preference in terms of assessment; males preferring exams and females preferring coursework. There have also been suggestions that GCSE and A'Levels favour coursework and so this explains the higher performance of females. However, there have been studies that have shown that this gender divide between assessments is no longer the case and female students perform equally well on exams and male students also show a personal preference

YEAR	FEMALE STUDENTS	MALE STUDENTS	DIFFERENCE (IN FAVOUR OF GIRLS)
2005/2006	63.9	54.3	9.6
2006/2007	66.0	57.0	9
2007/2008	69.9	60.9	9
2008/2009	74.5	65.8	8.7
2009/2010	79.0	70.8	8.2

Table 5.4 Percentages of students achieving 5+ GCSEs, grades A*–C
Source: Department for Education (2010).

Year	Males entered for 3 + A level	Females entered for 3 + A level	Males achieving 2 + A levels	Females achieving 2 + A levels
2006/2007	145,467	171,685	94.0	96.1
2007/2008	154,852	174,608	94.2	96.0
2008/2009	165,207	187,166	94.1	96.3
2009/2010	177,919	201,697	93.9	96.1

Table 5.5 Table of differences in entry and attainment regarding A'Levels
Source: Department for Education (2011).

for coursework (Elwood, 1999; Woodfield et al., 2005). It could be that the main area of difference stems from the fact that girls are more likely to find classes of interest and are also more likely to enjoy lessons (Gentry et al., 2002). These differences in educational attainment do not stop at A'Level, but continue beyond school and into higher education.

Gender and higher education

Historically it has been the case that more men went to university than women; however this trend has switched around with more women now attending university than men:

> The proportion of both men and women enrolling in college has increased since the 1970s, but the increase for women has been much more substantial. Trend statistics in the United States also reflect a striking reversal of a gender gap in college completion that once favoured males. In 1960, 65% of all bachelor degrees were awarded to men. Women continued to lag behind men in college graduation rates until 1982 when they reached parity with men. From 1982 onward the percentage of bachelor's degrees awarded to women continued to climb such that by 2005 women received 58% of all bachelor's degrees (Snyder & Dillow, 2007) and comprised 57% of all college students.
>
> (Buchmann et al., 2008, p. 325)

It is not just America that has witnessed this shift, but also the United Kingdom which now sees unprecedented numbers of students attending university; these students are disproportionately made up of young women as can be seen in Table 5.6:

Year	Male applicants	Female applicants	Difference
2005	238,664	283,491	44,827
2006	229,121	277,183	48,062
2007	240,904	293,591	52,687
2008	259,878	328,811	68,933
2009	284,757	355,103	70,346
2010	306,907	390,444	83,537

Table 5.6 University applicants according to gender, 2005–2010
Source: UCAS (2011).

Buchmann et al. (2008) suggest that there are a number of reasons for the increasing gender gap in higher education:

- Increased family level of education which in turn means that children are likely to be better educated
- Increased economic ability to attend university
- Higher educational aspirations of young women
- Increased number of female mature students
- The higher number of women in higher education is also likely to be related to the higher level of attainment shown by girls throughout their school careers
- Wider changes in the workplace which have reduced gender inequality (including changes to salaries)
- Improvements to gender role attitudes which are now more egalitarian

It is now of utmost importance that the gender gap does not continue to grow and that male students end up disadvantaged in the future.

◉ Chapter summary

In this chapter we have explored how gender affects adolescence, in terms of friendships, bullying, relationships, sex and education and it is clear that males and females have differing experiences of their teenage years. Males are more likely to have a larger and more diverse friendship group, but not a best friend, are more likely to engage in sexual intercourse earlier and do marginally worse at school than their female peers. Young women, on the other hand, have a smaller number of more intimate friendships, lose their virginity later and do better at school. There are also some negative experiences of adolescence, such as bullying (which tends to be more physical with boys and verbal with girls) and there is some tumult surrounding emerging sexualities, while the risks of unprotected sex and teenage parenthood also loom as young people become sexual adults. Thus there is a lot for an adolescent to consider and by this time in their lives their gender is a very distinct part of their identity and leads to varying experiences throughout their life course.

⊙ Further reading

Buchmann, C., DiPrete, T. A. & McDaniel, A. (2008). Gender inequalities in education. *Annual Review of Sociology, 34*, 319–337.

Tripp, J. & Viner, R. (2005). Sexual health, contraception and teenage pregnancy. *BMJ, 330*, 590–593.

⊙ Key search terms

Adolescence
Bullying
Gender and education
Romantic relationships
Teenage attitudes towards contraception
Teenage attitudes towards sex
Teenage pregnancy

Chapter 6

Psychoanalytic approaches

This chapter will look at psychoanalytic explanations of gender identity. Since its inception in Sigmund Freud's consultation room psychoanalysis has offered psychologists an alternative approach, one which presents the unconscious as the leading motivator behind our personality, our motivations and our behaviours. While psychoanalysis does have its critics (as with any psychological theory) it does have a lot to offer students and psychologists as it was one of the first approaches to successfully combine the social, the individual and the biological. While many of Freud's ideas regarding gender and sexuality are out-dated and drenched in the assumptions of a white middle-class man born in the 1800s, it can still help us in our approach to gender formation. There have also been many researchers who have followed and updated Freud's approach; we will also turn to one of these theorists, Erik Erikson, to further our notions of how gender identity is shaped. The dominant theories of both Freud and Erikson will be introduced, before we examine in detail how these theories shape our notions of gender.

This chapter will cover the following:

- Psychoanalytic structures: **Id**, **Ego** and **Superego**
- Freud's **Psychosexual Stages**
- The Oedipus and Electra complex
- Evaluation of Freud and gender
- Introduction to Erikson
- Erikson's **Psychosocial Stages**
- Evaluation of Erikson and gender

Sigmund Freud

We shall begin this exploration of Freud's theories (which are relevant to gender identity formation) by describing the structure of the mind according to psychoanalytic theory. Once this background knowledge has been covered, we will move on to consider the psychosexual stages as described by Freud, and then consider the Oedipus and Electra complexes.

Structure: Id, ego and superego

Freud argued that psychological processes occur within a mental structure which is comprised of the id, the ego and the superego. Each of these has a distinct character and purpose which will be described below. While these structures are not solely related to gender, they do appear throughout many psychoanalytic theories and so are worthy of a brief description at this juncture.

Id

The id is the primeval and innate aspect of our mental world and it is driven by the **pleasure principle** which aims to reduce tension, eliminate pain and consequently produce pleasure. The desires of an infant, for example, focus upon feeding: hunger leads to a build-up of psychic tension and physical discomfort and so the pleasure principle dictates that feeding must occur for comfort and pleasure to be achieved. In some cases this is managed through actual feeding, while at other times the drive is partially satiated by the use of a pacifier or by thumb-sucking (which produces the same sucking behaviour as feeding). The id is the most energetic of the structures which means that it is also able to relieve tensions by use of imagination, such as the use of a mental image of a bottle or breast. In young infants the id is the ruler of the psyche and babies are driven by the pleasure principle: their world is determined by their requirements for feeding, sleep and comfort, for example, which need to be satiated regardless of their environment or the other demands which may be placed on their caregivers. Thus the id is concerned with the satisfaction of drives and desires which is why it has been called the "spoiled child of the personality" (Hall, 1954, p. 27). In older infants, children and adults the demands of the id are regulated by the ego and superego; after all we would be unable to function on a social level if we were only concerned with our own pleasure principles and our own egocentric wants.

Ego

A newborn infant is very limited in its understanding of the world; due to the power and energy of the id they are unable to clearly discriminate between reality (such as actually feeding when hungry) and wish fulfilment through hallucinations (such as the imagined sucking on a bottle). As the child develops they begin to make this distinction that the imagined sucking on a bottle does not produce the warm sensation from being held whilst being fed by a caregiver, the sense of a satiated appetite or the taste of milk. This newly discovered boundary between reality and desire leads to the formation of the ego as it is the primary structure which deals with the demands of reality: Freud argued that "the ego's major functions were to represent reality and, through the erection of defenses, to channel and control internal drive pressures in the face of reality (including the demands of social convention and morality)" (Mitchell & Black, 1995, p. 24). Thus it is the role of the ego to manage the desires of the id according to the confines of reality. Freud described the ego in the following analogy:

> The ego's relation to the id might be compared to that of a rider to his horse. The horse supplies the locomotive energy, while the rider has the privilege of deciding on the goal and of guiding the powerful animal's movement. But only too often there arises between the ego and the id the not precisely ideal situation of the rider being obliged to guide the horse along the path by which it itself wants to go.
> (Freud, 1933/1964, p. 77, cited in Miller, 2011, p. 114)

Thus, developing at approximately two years of age, the ego is the mind's necessary control mechanism for the demanding and egocentric id.

Superego

While the id is present from birth and the ego develops very early on in life, the superego is the last of the mental structures to develop at approximately five to six years. The superego is the moral centre of the mind and develops in accordance with the rules and norms of society: it is the conscience. It matures following guidance from parents, teachers, communities and society as a whole as to what is acceptable and desirable behaviour. With this development the role of the ego becomes more strained as it fights not only to control the id's demands, but also fights to control them in accordance with the moral restraints imposed by the superego.

According to Freud these three structures form our personality, our self, our desires and our behaviours. While they do not relate to any particular brain regions, the structures are believed by psychoanalysts to form the basis of our mentality. The ego is the centre and works to balance the demands of the moral superego and the egotistic demands of the id; whilst doing this the ego is the structure which takes into the reality in which we operate our daily lives. These structures develop during childhood and occur during the child's increasing awareness that they are part of a larger world and that their desires are constricted by the confines of reality. Thus the development of the individual through childhood is central to the psychoanalytic perspective, particularly as it is also the period when an individual moves through the psychosexual stages which we will now turn to.

👁 Psychosexual stages

Freud proposed that a child progresses through several developmental stages which each focus the body's attention and libidinal drives towards a particular area of the body. Table 6.1 provides a brief overview of the psychosexual stages according to Freud.

According to Freud, between the ages of three and six children develop an interest in their genitals and the libidinal drives shift to focus on this erogenous zone. The presence of a penis, or absence in the case of girls, is of major concern to children during this stage and it is this presence or absence which leads to conflict. In boys this is known as the **Oedipus conflict** which, once resolved, leads to identification with the father; for girls the conflict is known as the **Electra conflict** and results in identification with the mother. Thus it is during this stage that children adopt gender-appropriate role models and begin to develop gender-appropriate behaviours. These conflicts will be explored in further detail in the next section.

STAGE	AGE	DESCRIPTION
Oral	Birth to 1 year	The infant's desires and pleasurable sensations are focused on the mouth, for example through sucking and feeding.
Anal	1 to 3 years	The toddler takes pleasure in its anus as it learns to regulate its defecation, i.e. through toilet training.
Phallic	3 to 6 years	Children develop an interest in their genitals and experience pleasure through masturbation. This is also the period then the Oedipus or Electra conflict is resolved and children learn to identify the same-sex parent.
Latency	6 years to adolescence	During this period the child shows little interest in sex and focuses its attention upon social relationships.
Genital	Adolescence to adulthood	This is the period when sexual desires develop into that of an adult and intimate relationships are formed.

Table 6.1 Freud's psychosexual stages

⊙ Oedipus and Electra conflicts

In this section we are going to examine the Oedipus and Electra complexes which Freud believed were conflicts every child must resolve:

> Based on listening to the fantasies of his patients and revealed by his own self-analysis was Freud's belief that all boys experience the unconscious wish to get rid of their father and replace him as mother's lover, and that all girls carry the unconscious wish to eliminate mother and replace her as father's lover. Because these fantasies are so dangerous and frightening, they are universally repressed; that is, they remain buried in the person's unconscious.
>
> (Kahn, 2002, p. 57–58)

These theories have elicited much attention over the years because they break two social taboos: incest (i.e. sexual attraction to a family member) and sexual desire experienced by children as we conceptualise children as being asexual (i.e. without sexual desire). Despite the controversy that surrounds them, they have remained integral to psychoanalytic theories of gender development: in order for a child to accept their same-sex parent (i.e. a girl accepting her mother, and boy his father) as their role model, they must overcome their Oedipus or Electra complex. We will now look at each one in more detail, beginning with Oedipus as Freud prioritised this conflict over the Electra conflict (described below) as he believed that the experience was more intense for boys.

The Oedipus myth

The Oedipus legend originates from Ancient Greece and is the tale of a young man who unwittingly killed his father and married his mother. The King of Thebes, Laius, had been told by an oracle that his son would kill him and take the Queen, Jocasta, as his wife; therefore he refrained from sexual intercourse with his wife, until one day he succumbed whilst inebriated. Still fearful of the oracle's warning he ordered his son be left alone on a mountainside; however a servant took pity on the small infant and passed him to a shepherd, rather than leave the infant to die. The infant was eventually given to, and raised by, the King and Queen of Corinth. As a young man Oedipus was warned by an oracle that his destiny was to kill his father and marry his mother. He misunderstood that the warning was in relation to the King and Queen of Corinth and so he decided to never return to Corinth and travelled to Thebes. On his way he got into a fight with a stranger who was travelling the other way; Oedipus killed the stranger and continued on his journey. Oedipus was unaware that this man was the King of Thebes and his biological father.

Upon reaching Thebes he discovered that the city was under the spell of a Sphinx who was devouring citizens who were unable to answer a riddle: 'What walks on four feet in the morning, two in the afternoon and three at night?' Oedipus was able to answer correctly: a human who crawls as an infant, walks as an adult, and uses a walking stick when elderly. In his anger at being answered correctly the Sphinx committed suicide, while Oedipus won the crown of Thebes and the hand of the widow Jocasta. Oedipus and Jocasta enjoyed a happy marriage, both ignorant of the truth behind their biological relationship, and had four children together. Several years later a dreadful plague took hold of Thebes and an oracle advised Oedipus that this was due to the city harbouring the murderer of Laius, who had to be found and punished before health and success would return to the city. At the same time Oedipus was advised that the King of Corinth had passed away and that he was adopted as an infant; it also emerged that Laius was killed on the roadside on a journey to Delhi to consult with the oracle there. These events led to the realisation that Oedipus had indeed killed his own father and married his mother, fatally fulfilling the oracle's prediction. Upon this realisation Jocasta committed suicide and Oedipus blinded himself. He was cast from Thebes and spent the remainder of his life wandering and being looked after by his daughter.

The Oedipus conflict

This ancient Greek myth gives its name to the psychoanalytic conflict Freud proposed which involves the attraction of boys to their mother which occurs during the phallic stage (see earlier in this chapter). The conflict begins with the role of the mother in the household; she is the primary provider of food, comfort and nurturance which creates the sense of a very powerful being. A young boy however sees an ally in his father against this power; in some ways in fact the father is more powerful than the mother. This sense of unity arises from a realisation on the part of the boy that both he and his father have a penis, whereas his mother does not. The penis therefore becomes a symbol of power and masculinity for the boy: his penis completes him both physically and mentally. Thus the conflict begins with the boy finding an ally in his father and recognising the power of his mother.

Once the boy understands how important a penis is, love for his mother becomes transformed into sexual desire and upon this transformation his father, formerly an ally, becomes a rival for his mother's affection. Freud and other psychoanalysts believe that this conflict can be eased or made more difficult by the attitude of the parents; for example a mother might joke about no woman ever being good enough for her son or a father might feel that he has been usurped by his son with regard to the mother's affections. Given the boy's conceptualisation of his father from ally into rival the boy becomes anxious that his father will act against him in a hostile way, specifically that his father will castrate him: thus the boy becomes consumed with **castration anxiety**. Freud argued that this specific anxiety regarding castration arises from the boy's realisation that girls' do not have a penis and his assumption that they must have previously had one and consequently have been castrated. In order to resolve this anxiety the boy realises that his sexual attraction for his mother is hopeless and instead seeks to identify himself with his powerful father. So during this period the boy learns to accept and identify with the same sex parent which is essential for his gender development. We will now move on to look at the female version of the Oedipus complex, the Electra conflict.

The Electra myth

Again the name of this conflict is taken from a Greek myth; Electra was the daughter of Agamemnon and Clytemnestra who were the King and Queen of Mycanae; she also had a younger brother, Orestes. Agamemnon left Mycanae for several years as he took part in the Trojan wars, during which time his wife took a lover, Aegisthus. When Agamemnon returned to Mycanae after an absence of many years he was murdered by Aegisthus and Clytemnestra. The lovers also plotted to murder Orestes, but Electra was able to save him; he was sent to the King Strophius who protected him and raised him alongside his own son, Pylades. When he reached adulthood Orestes returned to Mycanae in order to avenge his father's death. Before he committed the murders he visited his father's grave in order to perform death rites and pay his respect and it was here that he was reunited with Electra. She gave her blessing for the murder (and in some versions of the myth, was an accomplice too) and so Orestes murdered Aegisthus and Clytemnestra. He was assisted in the murders by Pylades who later married Electra.

The Electra conflict

The Electra conflict was named after this myth as it features a young girl whose love for her father shapes the rest of her life, which Freud theorised happened due to the Electra conflict. While there are many psychoanalytic writings on the Oedipus conflict, there is a relative scarcity of work regarding the Electra complex. This is arguably not only because Freud thought the Oedipus conflict was more intense, but also because "the female version of the Oedipus complex is less clearly worked out, in line with the fact that Freud continued to find women a puzzle through-out his life" (Storr, 1989, p. 24). The conflict begins in the same way as Oedipus, with the girl realising the power of her mother: her mother is the centre of her world. In order to create her own identity she must break free of her mother's power and turns to her father as a potential ally. She realises though that there is a separation between them due to their different anatomies; the lack of penis means that she can never be her father's comrade and so experiences **penis envy**. Freud wrote that:

> Little girls ... notice the penis of a brother or playmate, strikingly visible and of large proportions, at once recognize it as the superior

counterpart of their own small and inconspicuous organ, and from that time forward fall a victim to envy for the penis.

(Freud, 1925/2002, p. 16)

Thus she must find another way to create a strong bond with her father and she does this by realising that through a sexual relationship with her father she can, by implication, have possession of his penis and become his ally. She might also believe that the child resulting from intercourse with her father would fill the void that not having a penis has created for her. This desire for her father as a sexual being means that her mother is consequently positioned as a rival (as with the father in the Oedipus conflict). There is no easy resolution to this conflict, other than the girl's increasing awareness that other men are capable of providing her (through sexual ownership) with a penis and, ultimately, a baby. Thus by switching her attention to other men, she is able to repress the sexual desire for her own father, return to an affectionate (rather than adversarial) relationship with her mother and is able to identify with the same-sex parent which is how Freud theorised we come to learn how to be male or female. Unsurprisingly both the Oedipus and Electra conflicts have important implications for the development of gender which we will now address.

◉ Evaluation of Freud and gender

In the above section we have discussed how Freud conceptualised the Oedipus and Electra conflicts which occur during the phallic psychosexual stage. During this period boys experience sexual attraction towards their mothers and, consequently, resent their father due to jealousy. In time the child comes to realise that these feelings towards his mother are taboo and direct focus to their father; in this way boys come to accept their father as their role model. On the other hand girls realise that their mother is powerful and seek an allegiance with their father which, as this cannot be based on them both possessing a penis, is based upon sexual desire, which consequently positions the mother as rival. This conflict is resolved by the realisation that there are other men who are able to give the girl (by association) a penis and the consequent identification with the mother. Thus the conflicts involve a child experiencing sexual desire for the opposite gender parent, which resolves with a repression of this longing and an identification with the same-sex parent. These conflicts and their healthy resolution are essential to gender development as the child learns to identify with the same-sex parent and this is central when developing notions of what it is to be female or to be male. However, Freud's theorising often appears relatively limited under the glare of twenty-first century culture as the typical family described by Freud while common in the Edwardian period when he was writing, is by no means the only family structure that exists in contemporary society. How, for example, does the Oedipus or Electra conflict get played out in single-parent families where there might be no contact at all with the absent parent? Or in families where there are two parents of the same-sex?

⊙ Erik Erikson

Erikson's greatest contribution to psychology was his notion of psychosocial stages of development. The change in emphasis – Freud's psycho*sexual* stages and Erikson's psycho*social* stages – highlights the different areas of focus. Freud considered the **libido** the driving force behind the child's development, whereas Erikson, inspired by anthropology, believed that it is the wider social world and our relationships with others that are central to our progress. Table 6.2 briefly illustrates the stages as Erikson described them:

Stage	Age	Description
Trust vs. mistrust	Birth to 1 year	Infants must learn to trust and rely upon their caregivers to meet their needs; otherwise mistrust will be the basis of the relationship.
Autonomy vs. shame and doubt	1–3 years	During this stage children will learn to be autonomous and will begin to take care of themselves in some respects (such as during toilet training). If they do not acquire this skill then they will begin to doubt their own abilities.
Initiative vs. guilt	3–6 years	This stage sees the child begin to take control of their own world and their own activities: they develop a sense of independence. If they are not encouraged in this task then they will feel guilty for attempting to assert their independence.

Table 6.2 Erikson's psychosocial stages

Industry vs. inferiority	6–12 years	Children of this age are beginning to master socially approved skills and activities. A sense of inferiority may arise if children are unable to master such skills.
Identity vs. role confusion	12–18 years	Adolescents have many things to come to terms with, including a burgeoning body and sexual identity, and it is this stage where a sense of identity must be firmly established. If a notion of identity is not formed in this stage then they will be uncertain about their future.
Intimacy vs. isolation	18–30 years	Young adults must be able to form meaningful intimate relationships with others; otherwise they will risk isolation and loneliness.
Generativity vs. stagnation	30 to late adulthood	Adults are concerned with their productivity here, either in their careers or by developing the next generation (i.e. their children). If adults do not involve themselves in such production they will stagnate.
Integrity vs. despair	Late adulthood onwards	Older adults must come to terms with their accomplishments and disappointments; otherwise they will focus on their unfulfilled wishes and despair for lost opportunities.

Table 6.2 (Continued)

Thus we can see how Erikson's psychosocial stages offer the psychologist a comprehensive account of how identity develops throughout the life course. While drawing heavily upon Freud's psychosexual stages, Erikson positions the social as more important than the sexual and we can see the influence of personal relationships and the wider society in all of the psychosocial stages. What we are particularly interested in for the purposes of this text is the development of gender identity and Erikson's contribution to this field will now be explored.

◉ Psychosocial stages, identity and gender

Erikson's expansion and development of Freud's psychosexual stages have added much to psychoanalytical theorising and have improved the credibility of the psychoanalytic stages of development. While Erikson accepted much of what Freud said about the Oedipus and Electra conflicts he did not believe that the drive behind these conflicts was sexual, but was social. This did much to improve the credibility of psychoanalytic process of development as many were (and are still) uncomfortable with the notion of children as sexual beings, particularly if the desire is directed towards parents. Erikson's theory, with its focus on the social rather than the sexual, was thus more readily accepted. This focus on the social is very important in terms of gender because it is wider social conceptions of gender that shape our individual behaviours; for example 200 years ago it was unthinkable for women to receive a higher education but now, following changing notions of women's rights and capabilities, women are actively encouraged to reach university level education. By incorporating the social, rather than a focus on the biological, Erikson added much more weight and authority to the psychoanalytic understandings of how children develop into gendered beings.

Evaluation of Erikson and gender

There have been some criticisms of Erikson's stages of identity development by feminist writers who argue that Erikson positions the male sense of identity and identity formation as the 'normal' way of developing. Gilligan (1993) and Douvan and Adelson (1966) argue that identity is a different concept for each gender: men focus on the individual and occupational, whereas women focus on the interpersonal, that is their relationship with others is central to their identity. So, for example, when asked 'who are you?' a man might answer that he is a doctor, whereas a woman might answer that she is a mother, daughter, wife and friend. Erikson's theory rests on a notion of an individual identity and a sense of separateness which is a predominantly male sense of identity. Thus we have to be aware that there are limitations to the stages of identity formation as positioned by Erikson and that these limitations are a focus on the male rather than the female.

It should be noted that Erikson (1964) went someway to specifically address the psychology of women in an essay entitled 'Inner and outer space: Reflections on womanhood'. In this seminal work Erikson proposes that a woman "experiences her internal space as a fertile presence rather than an absence" (Mitchell & Black, 1995, p. 221). Thus the absence of a penis is not conceptualised as a weakness nor is the female body positioned as lacking due to this absence, rather the female body is described as just as powerful as that of a man. So we can see how Erikson has advanced a more sophisticated understanding of the female identity than Freud who remained fixated on the absence or presence of a penis with regard to gendered identities.

◉ Neo-Freudian approaches to gender

Since Freud there have been many more psychoanalytic theorists who are known as neo-Freudians. It is unsurprising, given the nature of some of Freud's claims regarding gender, that some of these psychoanalysts have developed more recent and contemporary notions of gender.

One of the first neo-Freudians to make a significant contribution to gender studies was Karen Horney (1885–1952) who was often critical of Freud's theories. She was particularly critical of his notion of penis envy (which was described earlier). She suggested that it was not the penis itself that some women were envious of, but the power that men possessed (Horney, 1923/1967, 1932). She also theorised that some men experience 'womb envy' as they experience jealousy regarding the fact that women can give birth and create life and men cannot. She discussed how the process of pregnancy, breastfeeding and motherhood as a whole made men feel inadequate and inspired them to establish their own power in different ways, such as economic power over women. This idea has been widely accepted in psychoanalysis and has been discussed and developed by many other writers since Horney (e.g. Klein, 1957; Riviere, 1937). In 2000 a historian named Robert McElvaine re-formulated 'womb envy' as 'non-menstrual syndrome' to refer to the envy by men of women's reproductive capabilities.

For Freud and some of his followers gender identity emerges solely from the anatomy of the individual and, most notably, the presence or absence of a penis. This has since been a point of criticism with Nancy Chodorow (1995) in particular emphasising the role of the cultural and personal in the shaping of gender identity. Furthermore Freud suggested that children learn from their parents about their gender, implying that those children from same-sex households (which are increasingly common in contemporary western society) would have an ill-adjusted gender identity. Research conducted by Susan Golombok (Golombok & Tasker, 1996; Golombok et al., 1983) which looked at households with lesbian parents or fatherless households has shown those children to be as well adjusted as those children raised in heterosexual households.

Thus we can see how a variety of neo-Freudians have advanced and improved upon Freud's original contributions to the consideration of gender formation. Freud's original works emerged from a Victorian notion of sex and gender when men were considered superior to women, intellectually, spiritually and corporeally. This is no longer a socially acceptable mindset in contemporary western society and the advances in psychoanalytical thought and gender reflect this change. Neo-Freudians now position women as equal to men (and in some cases superior due to their life-giving capabilities) and perceive libidinal drives as a contributory, but not a central factor in gender identity formation.

Evaluation of psychoanalytic approaches

Freud has come under fire over the years on several points concerning gender. Firstly there is the fundamental conceptualisation of the female body as 'missing' a penis. This not only presents the male body as the standard human form, but also positions the female body as deficient: specifically that the female body lacks the important penis. This, according to Freud, gives rise to penis envy: a concept in itself that many women (not just psychologists) take offence to. Secondly, Freud has consistently prioritised the male psyche over the female: the Oedipus complex, for example, is considered to be more important than the Electra conflict. This positioning of male over female is somewhat a product of its time; Freud was part of a patriarchal society where men were considered to be more important than women. This was a common belief at the turn of the twentieth century and had been so for several centuries in western society; therefore it is not surprising that this comes through in Freud's work. He was also writing at a time when science and society were embracing Darwin's notion of the survival of the fittest and the idea of biological destiny; thus gender was seen as predetermined by anatomy. However Freud's followers have come to understand gender and sexuality in very different ways and so there is a "contemporary rejection of Freud's presumption that both sexes assign a higher value inevitably and universally to masculinity, and that one's image of masculinity should provide the baseline to which femaleness is considered" (Mitchell & Black, 1995, p. 220). Thus for modern psychoanalysts the female form is seen as equal to the male form and we can understand gender identity as based on something much more complex than simply the absence or presence of a penis. There are several schools of analytic thought (such as Kleinian and Lacan) and each one has its own take on gender and gender identity, however each has developed and built upon Freud's notions of gender, sexuality and the Oedipal conflicts.

Given the strength and controversial nature of some of Freud's claims (such as the presence of penis envy in all women and the sexual desire of children for their parents) it would be easy to dismiss them out of hand. However, it has been said that a complete fool either accepts all of Freud's theories or denies all of Freud's theories. Freud's theories arose at a time when psychology was dominated by the experimental approaches of Wilhelm Wundt and his successors. Therefore the perspectives adopted by early psychologists were focused on outwardly measurable behaviour, whereas Freud proposed a radical change which sought to understand internal mental processes, motivations and drives behind our social behaviour and so "few educated people would fail to acknowledge that Freud has revolutionized our way of thinking" (Wolff, 1979, p. 355). Psychoanalytic techniques and theories have become part of our general cultural knowledge and are now a central tenet of much psychological theory and research.

As said earlier Freud's theories have been found wanting in light of modern notions of sexuality and gender. These shortcomings have been addressed by the work of neo-Freudians, such as Chodorow, Horney and Golombok, many of whom have taken Freud's original theories and developed them into socially and academically acceptable concepts. At the moment however psychoanalysis remains out of favour for many contemporary psychologists. Mainstream psychology is currently dominated by cognitive approaches and the actual process of psychoanalytic therapy remains a costly (in terms of both time and money) alternative to cognitive approaches. However, for the general public, Freud remains one of the most famous figures associated with psychology, and psychoanalytic therapy and its terms have become part of our popular culture.

◉ Chapter summary

In this chapter we have explored two predominant theories of identity development: Freud's psychosexual stages and Erikson's psychosocial stages. Freud argued that identity was the product of the interaction between the id, ego and superego and it developed in childhood through progression through the psychosexual stages. Identification with the same-sex parent, our predominant role model for how to 'be' male or female, comes about following the resolution of the Oedipus and Electra complexes: it is based on the feeling and consequent repression of sexual learning desire. While Erikson drew heavily upon Freud's theories, he was also influenced by anthropology and believed that it was social forces, rather than sexual forces, which were the driving force behind identity formation. In his psychosocial stages gender identity is not just shaped by the parent, as with Freud, and is also shaped by wider social forces, such as what a particular culture deems appropriate behaviour for a male and female. Thus in both theories being a 'girl' or being a 'boy' is not something that happens automatically for children, but is something that is arrived at through a process.

👁 Further reading

Mitchell, S. A. & Black, M. J. (1995). *Beyond Freud: A history of modern psychoanalytic thought*. New York: Basic Books.

👁 Key search terms

Castration anxiety
Ego
Electra conflict
Erik Erikson
Id
Oedipus conflict
Penis envy
Psychosexual stages
Psychosocial stages
Sigmund Freud
Superego

Chapter 7

Cognitive development theory

This chapter will focus primarily on the work of Kohlberg and his theories regarding gender development which draw heavily upon Piaget. We will focus this chapter on Kohlberg's three stages of gender development: **gender identity**, **gender stability** and **gender constancy**. This will provide a contrast to the psychoanalytical work covered in the previous chapter which sees the child as subject to libidinal drives and conflicts; whereas cognitive theories frame the child as an active participant in their development. In order to address these areas we will cover the following points:

- Kohlberg's cognitive-developmental theory of gender development
- Evaluation of Kohlberg's cognitive-developmental theory of gender development

👁 Lawrence Kohlberg

Kohlberg was heavily influenced by the work of Piaget as his most famous contribution to psychology, the development of moral stages, testifies. He, like Piaget, felt that a child's development was reliant upon cognitive development. This can be seen as a contrast to the psychoanalytic approaches of Freud and Erikson. According to Kohlberg's theorising the child is an active participant in their experience and they vigorously shape and alter their knowledge of the world. What is also crucial in Kohlberg's theories is the notion that the child's development is driven by its cognitive capability; a child cannot progress to the next developmental stage unless they are cognitively able. We will now look at each of Kohlberg's stages in more detail.

Thinking scientifically → **How do psychologists conduct research with very young children?**

Finding out about gender stereotypes from older children and adults is a relatively simple business – you can just ask them. However, this is not the case with very young children who have not yet mastered verbal language and so researchers have to use alternative ways of researching such issues. Some researchers look at visual preference, for example, as a measure of interest in infants (e.g. Campbell et al., 2000; Serbin et al., 2001). This technique has been further improved in recent years by developments in technology, as demonstrated by Alexander et al. (2009). Alternatively some researchers prefer to conduct observational studies to gauge an idea of the child's behaviour in their natural environment (such as Blakemore, 1990; Lamb et al., 1983). Thus there are a range of methods that are available to researchers to investigate psychological phenomenon in the very young.

Gender identity

This is the first stage that Kohlberg argued children must progress through and occurs around the age of 2–3 years. It is at this stage that a child correctly learns to identify him or herself as a boy or a girl. Thompson (1975) reports that at the age of 24 months 76 per cent of toddlers self-identified correct sex, this increased to 83 per cent at 30 months and 90 per cent at 36 months. Thus we can see that learning to identify sex, even our own, is a process that takes time; it is not a skill that we are born with, but something that we have to learn. At this initial stage the discrimination between genders is based on superficial characteristics, such as 'mummy is a girl because she has long hair' or 'daddy is a boy because he doesn't wear skirts'. There is also a lack of understanding that sex is fixed: if born a girl it is not possible to turn into a boy overnight or to change genders by adopting characteristics of the other sex (e.g. believing a man might turn into a woman if he wears skirts). Thus there is no real understanding of what gender is, but only that there are superficial characteristics associated with each gender (such as clothing and hairstyles).

👁 Gender stability

The next stage that a child must progress through is to understand that gender is stable and it is not something that can be easily changed. Children learn that girls grow up to be women and boys grow up to be men. This knowledge develops between the ages of three and seven. Thus children learn that their gender is an important and stable aspect of their identity.

👁 Gender constancy

This is the final stage of gender identity development according to Kohlberg which occurs between the ages of 7 and 12 and this is when children understand that their gender is constant, even in spite of superficial changes to appearance and behaviour. An older child should, for example, understand that a boy is able to dress as a girl and still remain a boy (and vice versa). This stage is strongly correlated with Piaget's concrete operational stage and the notion of constancy that he forwarded. Thus, just as the volume in the beaker remains the same even if the beaker changes shape, so gender remains constant despite superficial changes in appearance.

Kohlberg placed particular emphasis upon this final stage and the concept of gender constancy. He argued that once a child has understood what it is to be male or female, they will then start **modelling** their behaviour on same-sex role models. Thus once a child has realised he is a boy and will remain male, then he will turn to fellow men, such as his father and male friends at school, to learn gender appropriate behaviours and activities. What is most important in this is the order: the child realises he is male and then turns to male role models. This process is termed 'self-socialisation' by Maccoby and Jacklin (1974). This is a process that is separate to parental or social influences acting upon the child, but instead involves the child actively choosing to mimic the gendered behaviour of others: during self-socialisation the child itself is the driving force.

One famous study that has been used in support of Kohlberg's theory of gender constancy was conducted by Slaby and Frey in 1975. They assessed 55 children aged between 2 and 5 years in order to evaluate their knowledge and understanding of gender. They asked the children a series of questions which assessed the three levels; below are some examples of these questions:

Gender Labelling: Is this doll a boy or a girl?
Are you a boy or a girl?
Gender Stability: When you were younger, were you a boy or a girl?
When you grow up will you be a mummy or a daddy?
Gender Constancy: Could you be a boy if you wanted to be? (asked to a girl)
Could you be a girl if you wanted to be? (asked to a boy)

They found that the majority of children were able to correctly identify their own sex by the age of three, but that a clear sense of gender constancy did not begin to emerge until around age five. They also showed children a short film (with both male and female actors) a few weeks after the initial round of questioning and found that children who scored higher on gender constancy paid more attention to the same-sex actor. They concluded that the results of their study showed that:

> ... young children's perception of their own gender similarity to an adult model may develop in stages in conjunction with their cognitive understanding that gender is a constant human attribute.
>
> (Slaby & Frey, 1975, p. 854)

Thus the more aware children were of gender constancy, the more likely they were to pay attention to same sex models. There is some argument however that the questions asked by Slaby and Frey (1975) are confusing and can be open to different interpretations and also that the questions do not involve a visual transformation and so are inadequate in terms of a Piaget style conservation task; what these problems mean is that the results could have produced an artificially high result for the number of children who have reached gender constancy (Bem, 1989).

⊙ Evaluation of Kohlberg and gender

Kohlberg's (1966) stages of gender development have been accepted for the large part as they have been substantiated with evidence from other researchers. A study by Damon (1977) has been much cited, for example, as providing support for Kohlberg's hypotheses. Damon (ibid.) conducted research with 4- to 9-year-olds and gave them a hypothetical scenario which tested their understanding of gender identity, stability and constancy. Damon talked to the children about a little boy called George who enjoyed playing with dolls and then asked them a series of questions (such as whether George was right to play with dolls) and looked at their responses to gain an insight into the child's understanding of gender. Younger children (aged four) displayed no concern regarding the gender associated nature of the play; they simply replied that George should play with dolls if he wanted to. Older children (aged six) reacted negatively to George's play behaviour and argued that he should not be playing with dolls as girls play with dolls, not boys. The oldest of the children questioned (aged nine) did not feel as strongly as the six-year-olds; they felt that it was unusual for a boy to want to play with dolls, but that George should still be allowed to play with them if he wanted to. Thus this study provided empirical evidence for supporting Kohlberg's claims of stages in gender development, most significantly at the stage of gender constancy when children are aware that there are gender-appropriate behaviours, but that these behaviours can be performed by the opposite sex without creating a long-term threat to gender identity.

While there is evidence to suggest that Kohlberg was correct regarding the stages of gender development, there is some research that suggests that Kohlberg was incorrect regarding the ages at which this development occurs. Certainly there is substantial evidence suggesting that children are more aware of gender and gender-appropriate objects and behaviours much earlier than Kohlberg indicates. In a recent study this has been shown to occur as young as 18 months in girls (Serbin et al., 2001), with toddlers matching male or female faces to male or female associated toys (such as a female face matching with a doll and a male face matching with a truck). While another study by the same authors (Poulin-Dubois et al., 2002) has shown that infants aged 24 months demonstrate some awareness of gendered tasks. This study involved a researcher engaging in play in front of the child; a gender-neutral stuffed toy (a monkey) used props to perform imitations of household tasks. A third of these tasks are considered masculine (such as fixing the car), a third as feminine (such as putting on make-up) and a third as gender-neutral (such as drinking from a cup). Once this had been modelled for the child, the toddler was asked to play as well. However, instead of having a gender-neutral soft toy, the toddler had two dolls (one male and one female) and had to select one of the dolls to perform the task. Nearly three-quarters (73 per cent) of the girls used the gender-appropriate doll to perform the gender-appropriate tasks, however just under half of the boys did this (a finding that is statistically insignificant as it is attainable by chance alone). Thus while there were some differences between the toddlers' results, this study does indicate that already children (particularly females) demonstrate a much greater awareness of gender-roles and gender-appropriate behaviours than Kohlberg (1966) would indicate is possible at this age.

There is some evidence to suggest that children demonstrate a 'pseudo-constancy' period around the age of four. At this age children are likely to give the correct response to multiple choice questions regarding the constancy of gender. In a well-cited study Bem (1989) showed children aged three and four years photographs of nude toddlers: one male and one female. Children were able to correctly identify males and females based on external genitalia, thus displaying some knowledge of the anatomical basis of gender. What was somewhat surprising was that children were then able to correctly name the sex of the toddler even if the toddler was photographed wearing gender-inappropriate clothing; so children who had been shown the nude photograph of the male toddler then went on to identify him as still being a boy even when the photograph showed him wearing a dress. Thus preschool children gave answers that suggested they were aware gender remained constant based on anatomy, which is in opposition to Kohlberg's (1966) supposition. This early appearance of an understanding of gender constancy has been evidenced elsewhere (e.g. Emmerich et al., 1977) and has been termed 'pseudo-constancy' (Eaton & Von Bargen, 1981). This does appear to be a temporary display of understanding and is arguably related to methodology selection as children who answer correctly to a multiple-choice response are unable to verbalise their reasoning behind their choice.

Additionally it has been suggested that this 'pseudo-constancy' is the result of an understanding of categories, rather than knowledge of gender constancy; so the children who respond that the toddler is still a boy (even though he is wearing a dress) might be drawing upon the earlier category they had already assigned to the toddler (Martin et al., 2002).

Furthermore there is some debate regarding the role of the social in cognitive development. The underlying assumption of cognitive theories (such as work by Kohlberg and Piaget) is that the social development of a child is driven by its cognitive capabilities, but there is evidence to suggest that perhaps it is the social that drives the cognitive development of the child (most famously by Vygostky, 1986). There is no clear way to assess which comes first, the cognitive or the social, and this remains something of a 'chicken or the egg' scenario for developmental researchers. An indication of this debate can be seen in a study by La Freniere et al. (1984) which looked at the interactions between children in a day-care centre and found that by the age of two female toddlers were demonstrating a significant preference for same-sex peers, while boys were displaying this same preference by the age of three years. Thus this preference for interactions with same-sex peers has been shown to occur much earlier than self-socialisation (Maccoby & Jacklin, 1974) would suggest which posits that children must have a cognitive model of what it is to be male or female before self-selecting peers of the same gender. Thus it becomes difficult to assess whether the same-sex preference (i.e. the social) is driven by knowledge of gender identity (i.e. the cognitive), or whether the development of gender-identity understanding (the cognitive) is driven by the association with same-sex peers (the social).

◉ Chapter summary

In this chapter we have explored an approach that argues that the development of gender is not driven by personal drives or social factors but is driven by the child's own cognitive development. In these terms a child has to cognitively understand what it is to be male or female, before it can actually learn to be male or female. This understanding is driven by the child's cognitive capabilities; they are unable to understand the complexities of gender constancy, for example, until they are capable of mastering concrete or formal operations (as described by Piaget). Thus the child is the active driver of their gender development, rather than a passive recipient.

While there is evidence to support Kohlberg's (1966) suggestion of a stage theory of gender identity development, it is clear that there are still some on-going debates around the topic, particularly the role of the social in cognitive development (much as there remains a similar debate regarding theories by Piaget). There have been attempts to bring together the social and cognitive, and this is something that is attempted by the gender **schema** theory which is the focus of the next chapter.

Further reading

Kohlberg, L. (1966). A cognitive–developmental analysis of children's sex-role concepts and attitudes. In E. E. Maccoby (Ed.). *The development of sex differences* (pp. 82–172). Stanford, California: Stanford University Press.

Martin, C. L., Ruble, D. N. & Szkrybalo, J. (2002). Cognitive theories of early gender development. *Psychological Bulletin, 128*(6), 930–933.

Key search terms

Cognitive development
Gender stability
Gender constancy
Lawrence Kohlberg
Self-socialisation
Piaget's cognitive stages

Chapter 8

Gender schema theory

This chapter will look at an approach which focuses more on the social aspects of cognitions regarding gender; specifically how the formation of gender schemas impact upon the child's development of a gendered identity. The theory draws heavily upon Kohlberg's (1966) description of the cognitive development of gender as it also places the child as an active participant in the development of their own gender. However, the gender schema theory (Bem, 1981a; Martin & Halverson, 1981) suggests that this development can occur with a much more simplistic level of understanding and can even begin in infancy. The gender schema theory also highlights the cultural nature of the developing cognitions as these cognitions are based on gender schemas and stereotypes which are social.

In this chapter we will explore the following points:

- Description of the **Bem Sex Role Inventory** (BSRI)
- Evaluation of the current validity of the BSRI
- Introduction to schemas
- Description and evaluation of the gender schema theory

👁 Bem's Sex Role Inventory

In 1974 Bem published her Sex Role Inventory (BSRI) which was important in that it positioned masculine and feminine traits as two independent dimensions (i.e. similar to a graph which has an X and a Y axis). This was in contrast to previous thinking which had positioned masculinity and femininity as two end points on the same continuum (i.e. just one axis). The predominant shortcoming of positioning masculinity and femininity on the same axis was that it denied individuals the opportunity to be conceptualised as both masculine and feminine, for example a woman might be nurturing at home, but in the workplace she may be very ambitious. Bem argued that an inventory that looked at both dimensions (rather than just focusing on either masculinity or femininity) would allow the individual to be assessed as either masculine, feminine or androgynous based on the interaction between the dimensions. Importantly the BSRI also used measures that reflected the cultural ideas of gender (i.e. in America in the early 1970s), rather than looking at measures that the participant considered to be masculine or feminine. Thus the scale attempts to tap into culturally defined gender schemas (see below for a definition of gender schemas) and how the individual rates themselves against these gender stereotypes.

The BSRI consists of a 60-item list of personality traits and characteristics; 20 of which are masculine traits, 20 feminine and 20 neutral. These can be seen in Table 8.1.

The scale is very easy for the participant to complete; they simply have to rate themselves (on a scale of one to seven) as to how socially desirable the list items are. Upon completion the participant will end up with a

MASCULINE	FEMININE	NEUTRAL
Acts as a leader, aggressive, ambitious, analytical, assertive, athletic, competitive, defends own beliefs, dominant, forceful, has leadership abilities, independent, individualistic, makes decisions easily, masculine, self-reliant, self-sufficient, strong personality, willing to take a stand, and willing to take risks	Affectionate, cheerful, childlike, compassionate, does not use harsh language, eager to soothe hurt feelings, feminine, flatterable, gentle, gullible, loves children, loyal, sensitive to the needs of others, shy, soft spoken, sympathetic, tender, understanding, warm, and yielding	Adaptable, conceited, conscientious, conventional, friendly, happy, helpful, inefficient, jealous, likable, moody, reliable, secretive, sincere, solemn, tactful, theatrical, truthful, unpredictable, and unsystematic

Table 8.1 Examples of items from the Bem Sex Role Inventory (1974)

score for masculinity, femininity and **androgyny** which range from one to seven. It is the androgyny score that is of particular importance as this gives an indication as to the relativity of the masculinity and femininity scores as Bem notes:

> It should be noted that the greater the absolute value of the Androgyny score, the more the person is sex typed or sex reversed, with high positive scores indicating femininity and high negative scores indicating masculinity. A 'masculine' sex role thus represents not only the endorsement of masculine attributes but the simultaneous rejection of feminine attributes. Similarly, a 'feminine' sex role represents not only the endorsement of feminine attributes but the simultaneous rejection of masculine attributes. In contrast, the closer the Androgyny score is to zero, the more the person is androgynous. An 'androgynous' sex role thus represents the equal endorsement of both masculine and feminine attributes.
>
> (1974, pp. 158–159)

The BSRI therefore attempts to provide an individual score relating to an individual's reported conformity to the cultural schemas of masculinity and femininity. While there are on-going debates regarding the validity of the measure (see evaluation later on in the chapter) the measure has been widely adopted by researchers, particularly the shorter version of the BSRI (Bem, 1981b).

Children's Sex Role Inventory

In 1991 Boldizar re-configured the BSRI (1974) into a measure that could be used with children, thus providing researchers with a method of assessing the level of **sex typing** occurring in childhood. In order to do this she designed phrases instead of using the terms from the BSRI (1974) which then enabled the children to rate their own traits. Several examples of these statements can be seen in Table 8.2.

The children were asked to rate on a four-point scale (rather than a seven-point scale) how well these statements applied to them. Changing the measure in this way made the scale easier to understand as the children were dealing with self-assessments, rather than assessing social desirability at a more abstract level (as in the BSRI).

The CSRI (Boldizar, 1991) has since been recognised as a valid and reliable measure of sex typing in children. It has, for example, been used

SUBSCALE	CSRI ITEM	BSRI ITEM
Feminine	I can usually tell when someone needs help	Sensitive to the needs of others
	I like babies and small children a lot	Loves children
	I am a kind and caring person	Tender
Masculine	When I play games, I really like to win	Competitive
	I like to think about and solve problems	Analytical
	I am sure of my abilities	Self-reliant
Neutral	I am an honest person	Sincere
	I like to help others	Helpful
	I always do what I say I will do	Reliable

Table 8.2 Comparison of the CSRI (Boldizar, 1991) and BSRI (Bem, 1974)

to look at the relationship between gender and perceived self-competence (Rose & Montemayor, 1994), the association between gender and levels of fearfulness and anxiety (Ginsburg & Silverman, 2000; Palapattu et al., 2006) and pain reactions (Myers et al., 2006).

One important feature of the CSRI is that it was only designed to be used with older children (approximately aged 9 and older). While this is an understandable limitation (so, for example, younger children might have difficulty understanding some of the questions) it does limit the application of the measure; for example while it might be interesting to carry out a longitudinal study using the CSRI to see how the results varied as the child aged, it would only be possible to do this once the child was old enough. There are further criticisms that can be levelled against the CSRI, but these also apply to the BSRI which is evaluated in the next section.

👁 Evaluation of the BSRI

As with all psychological measures there have been some criticisms of the BSRI, the most enduring criticism being that its validity is limited somewhat because it focuses on gender schemas from a very particular culture (America in the 1970s). Since that period monumental changes have been made in addressing gender inequality (although arguably there is still some way still to go) and we have since witnessed the third wave of

2005) and Japan (Katsurada & Sugihara, 1999). Thus there still remains debate as to whether the BSRI (Bem, 1974) is a valid measure of masculinity and femininity, but this appears to be reliant upon the cultural stereotypes regarding gender held by the local community. Thus the BSRI (Bem, 1974) is a useful measure of cultural notions of masculinity and femininity, but must be used with caution as a researcher should not assume that gender stereotypes are universal when research demonstrates that they are culturally specific.

◉ BSRI and gender schema theory

As described earlier the BSRI 'attempts to provide an individual score relating to an individual's reported conformity to the cultural schemas of masculinity and femininity'. However, it does not explain how an individual might come to view the world and themselves according to gender schemas. In order to rectify this Bem (1981a) suggested the gender schema theory to suggest how this process might take place. Although this might have been a logical progression in terms of Bem's research the move has been criticised in the past. Spence and Helmreich (1981), for example, argue that the BSRI is better regarded as a measure of expressiveness and instrumentality rather than a global measure of gender schemas. However, despite such criticisms the gender schema theory remains an important contribution to the study of gender development.

◉ Gender schema theory

Before we move on to explore the gender schema theory (Bem, 1981a) it is essential that we clarify what is meant by schemas.

Schemas

This is a term predominantly used in social psychology and refers to "a mental structure which contains general expectations and knowledge of the world. This may include general expectations about people, social roles, events and how to behave in certain situations" (Augoustinos & Walker, 1995, p. 32). This basically means that as we learn about the world we create expectations about certain places, peoples and events. If you were thinking of taking a holiday to Venice in Italy (even if you have never visited before), you would have a certain idea as to what to expect: you would think about a trip on a gondola with a gondolier dressed in a striped top and straw hat, you would imagine the beautiful architecture, perhaps even some specific artworks, you would think about the food that Venice is famous for and even imagine drinking an espresso in the busy Piazza San Marco. Thus we have expectations about events, places and people we have never encountered before.

There are many types of schemas, but we shall briefly explore just four: person schemas, self schemas, role schemas, and event schemas (also known as scripts). *Person schemas* are general ideas that we form about particular people, which may be a familiar person (such as a friend or relative) or someone unknown to us (such as a celebrity or a member of a group or profession). We might have an idea that Grandma likes baking and knitting or that a particular celebrity is a fan of yoga and leads a teetotal lifestyle or we might associate personality traits to a particular vocation (e.g. we might consider bankers to be greedy and accountants to be boring). A *self schema* refers to ideas and expectations that we have of ourselves, we might consider ourselves to have certain personality traits, characteristics, weaknesses and abilities; given our in-depth knowledge, our self-schemas are also more detailed than person schemas we might hold about other people. *Role schemas* are expectations we have about the roles people might adopt: we would expect a doctor, for example, to ask us intimate questions about our bodies and habits and we would expect a waiter to ask us what we would like to eat. These schemas are often related to *event schemas* or *scripts* which are general ideas related to certain events or processes. We know that when we go to the cinema the film will start at a specified time, we know that we might eat particular foods and we know that we are expected to be quiet while watching the film. Similarly we know that when we attend a class we are expected to sit in a particular place and the teacher will also stand in a particular place, we know we are expected to take notes and to listen and we know we are expected to raise our hands if we want to ask a question rather than just shout out. These schemas are also subject to *cognitive availability*, that is the readiness at which these expectations are at hand; for example, if your friend was describing a holiday and talked of long sandy beaches with clear blue sea you might assume that they had travelled abroad rather than to a beach in the United Kingdom.

Thus we have particular ideas and expectations about people, places, roles, jobs, events and ourselves that shape how we approach these experiences.

Gender schema theory

We obviously also have a multitude of schemas regarding genders: we might expect certain vocations to be associated with a particular gender (fire-fighters with males and nurses with females, for example), we might associate personality traits with genders (men as protective and women as nurturing) and thousands of other small, daily interactions that differentiate between masculine and feminine. Unsurprisingly these schemas are closely related to stereotypes which are a "widely shared and simplified evaluative image of a social group and its members" (Hogg & Vaughan, 2005, p. 584). While there are stereotypes and schemas regarding every category of person those concerned with gender are particularly prevalent:

> Clearly the developing child is learning content-specific information, the particular behaviours and attributes that are to be linked with sex. In most societies, this is a diverse and sprawling network of associations encompassing not only those features directly related to male and female persons, such as anatomy, reproductive function, division of labor, and personality attributes, but also features more remotely or metaphorically related to sex, such as the angularity or roundedness of an abstract shape and the periodicity of the moon. Indeed, there appears to be no other dichotomy in human experience with as many entities assimilated to is as the distinction between male and female.
>
> (Bem, 1981a, p. 354)

Thus not only do we assign gender attributes to people, personalities and tasks, but we also allocate them to shapes (think of an hourglass, for example), colours (blue and pink) and features of the natural world (the sun is traditionally thought of as masculine and the moon as feminine) and so gender is, literally, everywhere.

It is also crucial to understand that these schemas and stereotypes are a by-product of that particular social environment. This is something we will explore more in the final chapters, but it is also important to emphasise this point here. Bem writes of "society's cultural definitions of femaleness and maleness" (1983, p. 603) and so a child growing up in Britain in the twenty-first century will have a very different notion of masculine and feminine than a child growing up in India in the twenty-first century or Britain in the seventeenth century because the "*cultural definitions*" will differ. By focusing on gender schemas, which are social and cultural, it is clear that this theory of gender development is more strongly associated with the social than the cognitive theory of Kohlberg which was discussed in the previous chapter.

The acquisition of gender schemas begins during infancy and there is some evidence to suggest that development is particularly rapid between the ages of 2 and 3 years (Campbell et al., 2004), with children first developing a schema regarding the physical differences between the sexes (Barberá, 2003). Tautner et al. (2005) suggest that there are three stages during which gender schemas become integrated into cognitive models:

1 BEGINNING OF AWARENESS
  During the preschool years (approximately age 2–3 years) children learn to develop notions of gendered characteristics, behaviours and personality traits (i.e. gender schemas). This has been shown to begin during early infancy (see Chapter 3 for a discussion of gender awareness and development in infancy) and development seems to occur rapidly between the ages of 2 and 3.

2 RIGIDITY
  This knowledge is organised into very strict gender schemas which display no flexibility and the peak of these rigid notions of gender occurs at approximately 5–7 years of age. During this stage there appears to be an 'either or' approach; so, for example, 'only girls can wear pink' or 'only boys can be builders' are comments that we might expect to hear from children of this age.

3 FLEXIBILITY
  Finally during the concluding stage regarding gender schemas (around 7 years of age) there emerges a flexibility to these rigid notions of gender; so children learn to realise that boys can wear pink and have long hair or that women can also be builders or astronauts.

Once these gender schemas have become internalised the child then begins to use these as a marker of their own behaviour, that is once the child realises how girls are supposed to be nurturant or how boys are supposed to be adventurous, they will develop this aspect of themselves. Bem writes:

> The gender schema becomes a prescriptive standard or guide, and self-esteem becomes its hostage. Here, then, enters an internalized motivational factor that prompts an individual to regulate his or her behavior so that it conforms to cultural definitions of femaleness and maleness.
>
> (1983, p. 605)

So the gender schemas are used by the child to regulate their behaviour in order to achieve culturally acceptable notions of femininity and masculinity. So, for example, Martin and Halverson (1981) describe how children, when approaching a gendered object (such as a doll or a truck), refer to schemas and their own gender to ascertain whether the toy is relevant to them; so a boy might be presented with a toy truck, remember that 'trucks are for boys' and that, as he is a boy, the toy is appropriate for him to play with. Thus the gender schema theory works by focusing the child's attention on gender appropriate objects, activities and behaviours on gender appropriate schemas, which then act to reinforce the schema.

Thinking scientifically → **Gender and colouring books**

So where do we get our ideas about gender? One avenue through which we receive information about gender is the print media and while research has been often conducted looking at the depictions of gender stereotypes in children's story books (e.g. Turner-Bowker, 1996), newspapers (e.g. Knight & Giuliano, 2001) and advertising (e.g. Goffman, 1979) there has been little research conducted on the portrayals of men and women within colouring books, yet *"it would be rare for a young child not to be exposed to a coloring book"* (Fitzpatrick & McPherson, 2010, p. 127). In a 2010 study Fitzpatrick and McPherson conducted a study which looked at 56 randomly selected colouring books which featured 889 characters. Of these 889 there were 436 male figures and 306 females (147 characters were either of an unclear gender or were not gendered at all (such as a building with a smiling face)). Of these gendered figures, the authors report that:

- Male characters were more prevalent than female characters, but these characters were more likely to be animal figures than human figures.
- The male figures were more likely to be shown being active, while the females were more likely to be depicted in static positions.
- Males were also much more likely to be depicted as superheroes than female figures (90 per cent vs. 10 per cent).
- Furthermore males were more likely to be featured as adults, and females as children.

The prevalence of male figures is of note as this has been consistently reported elsewhere with regard to media (e.g. Signorielli et al., 1994; Turner-Bowker, 1996) and it may be that *"quantity often implies importance, especially to an impressionable mind. Seeing more of the other gender may lead young girls to view themselves as less important or as second-class citizens"* (Fitzpatrick & McPherson, 2010, p. 134). The researchers also found a skew in the presence of gender stereotypes in the colouring books aimed at girls, therefore suggesting that young girls were more exposed to these images than boys. Thus there is evidence that children are regularly faced with stereotypical images which act to strengthen their developing gender schemas (Bem, 1981a). Fitzpatrick and McPherson's study (2010) provides evidence that even in the twenty-first century young children are being presented with the notion that males are more active, more prevalent and more powerful than females who are featured as childlike, passive and vulnerable.

According the gender schema theory the child assimilates information regarding gender schemas and so learns what it is to 'be' male or female, feminine or masculine. It is this knowledge of 'maleness' and 'femaleness' that is tested by the BSRI (1974). Bem proposed the gender schema theory (1981a) as an advance on the BSRI. She suggested (through the gender schema theory) that how individuals behave is dependent upon how central they consider gender schemas to be; thus while the BSRI categorised individuals as masculine or feminine, the gender schema theory proposes that individuals are schematic (i.e. conform strongly to gender schemas) or aschematic (i.e. are not concerned with gender schemas).

Thinking scientifically → **Contributors to gender schema theory**

Martin and Halverson's (1981) book was published in the same year as Bem's (1981) which laid out the foundation for the gender schema theory and Martin and Halverson put forward a very similar argument. Thus it should be acknowledged that Bem is not the only significant proponent of a gender schema theory, and Carol Lynn Martin has also written extensively on the topic (e.g. Martin, 1989; Martin, 1993; Martin & Ruble, 2004). The focus in this chapter has remained on Bem's work as this enabled us to also consider the BSRI (Bem, 1974), the CSRI (Boldizar, 1991) and the Enculturated Lens Theory (Bem, 1993) in more detail.

In her 1983 paper Bem sets forward suggestions as to how parents might attempt to raise gender-aschematic children within a culture that is gender-schematic itself. This is a deep personal conviction of her own; she and her former husband worked hard to instil a sense of gender equality in their children and consider themselves to have been successful in raising their three children in a gender-aschematic way (Bem, 2001). She (1983) suggests that the first step in parents accomplishing this is to run their household in an aschematic manner: so household chores are participated in equally, not designating specific chores according to gender (as they would be in schematic households) such as DIY (traditionally a male task) and childcare (traditionally a female domain). Bem (1983) also suggests teaching children that the sexes are divided according to anatomy only and describes how this was done with her own children:

> Accordingly, when our children asked whether someone was male or female, we frequently denied certain knowledge of the person's sex, emphasizing that without being able to see whether there was a penis or a vagina under the person's clothes, we had no definitive information. Moreover, when our children themselves began to utilize nonbiological markers as a way of identifying sex, we gently teased them about that strategy to remind them that the genitalia and only the genitalia constitute the definition of sex: 'What do you mean that you can tell Chris is a girl because Chris has long hair? Does Chris's hair have a vagina?'.

> (Bem, 1983, p. 612–613)

Thus she argues that it is possible to raise children in an aschematic way, but that this does require parents to actively combat the schematic nature of contemporary society.

Enculturated lens theory

Bem referred to the subscription to gender schemas as the way in which an individual was willing to view the world and their experiences through the lens of gender which gave rise to the title of her 1993 book *The Lenses of Gender*. Thus an individual's position on the BSRI (1974) scale is heavily influenced by their schematic conformity; so a woman who is strongly schematic is likely to score highly with regard to her femininity on the BSRI. However, Bem attempted to progress her gender schema theory by drawing attention to the cultural environment in which gender schemas arise.

Bem (1993) argues that there are a number of set assumptions in society and these assumptions affect how we perceive gender in daily interactions and events. Bem referred to these as 'lenses' (as we view the world through them) and argued that there are three principal lenses in modern America:

THE LENS OF GENDER POLARISATION
This is similar to the gender/sex binary discussed earlier in the book which refers to the notion that there are only two sexes: male and female. On the basis of this division individuals are treated differently according to their sex and their social lives are consequently different too. This happens at an early age (even before birth) where male infants are associated with the colour blue and girls with the colour pink. Also children's activities are arranged on the basis of gender, from play (either with dolls or with toy cars) and organised activities (such as a boy playing in a football team and a girl attending ballet lessons).

THE LENS OF ANDROCENTRISM
This lens presents the male perspective as prioritised in American culture. It is also stated that the male stance is the standard against which women are judged (often unfavourably); so, for example, being rational (traditionally associated with males) is prioritised over being emotional (traditionally associated with females). Bem (1993) states that this prioritisation of male is also reflected in the English language, in the legal system and theology.

THE LENS OF BIOLOGICAL ESSENTIALISM

Finally this third lens refers to the frequent attempts to reduce the differences between the genders to mere biology. This serves to reinforce male power by asserting that the differences arise from anatomy, rather than social structures.

There have been criticisms that the enculturated lens theory fails to account for gender differences in individual situations (Deaux, 1994) with too great a focus on the macro level. Bem (1994) responds to this criticism stating that the lack of focus on the micro level is a deliberate feature of the theory; to quote her: "theorizing about the social reproduction of male power in U.S. society-a phenomenon, I assert, in which the internalization of cultural lenses and the self-construction of identity in terms of those lenses are critical" (ibid., p. 98). Thus the theory is an attempt to understand why male power is predominant in western societies (particularly in the United States) and why this power imbalance continues to be reproduced generation after generation.

◉ Evaluation of gender schema theory

Drawing on the widely held notion that humans, particularly as they are developing, have a predisposition to organise information into meaningful categories, the gender schema theory has attracted many proponents over the years. However, gender schemas are not just categories that are blindly accepted by the child, but are categories that are dynamically built and created by the child. This constructs the child as an active participant in their own development which is one of the great strengths of this theory. This also allows for variation (both personal and cultural) in gender schemas, although this variation is something of an under-researched area (Martin et al., 2002).

One of the major flaws with the gender schema theory is that it fails to take into account the anatomy of the child. As we discussed earlier biology is not the only factor regarding sex and gender, but it is an important one that should be considered. Having a male or female body has a significant influence on our psychological perceptions regarding gender and this should not be overlooked. During puberty, for example, perceptions of sex, sexuality and gender become irrevocably connected to the developing adult form and reproductive capabilities. However, the corporeal body is not considered within the gender schema theory and the crucial period of puberty is neglected. Similarly a focus on the social aspects of gender schemas is lacking and the focus has remained on the internal and cognitive processes (Martin et al., 2002); although Bem's later advancement of the enculturated lens theory goes someway to addressing this flaw. Overall however gender schema theory has made a positive contribution to our understanding of gender development and still offers researchers a solid foundation for research.

◉ Chapter summary

In this chapter we have explored the gender schema theory (Bem, 1981a; Martin & Halverson, 1981) which is influenced by the cognitive theory of gender development discussed in the previous chapter (Kohlberg, 1966). However, there is a significant difference between the theories as described by Martin and Ruble:

> Kohlberg's theory emphasized the active role of the child in gender development, and proposed that children's understanding of gender concepts influences their behavior, and that this influence becomes more pronounced once children reach a relatively sophisticated understanding of gender – knowing that a person's sex is stable and unchanging. In the 1970s, a new group of cognitive approaches to gender emerged – gender-schema theories. Gender schema theory is based on the idea that children form organized knowledge structures, or schemas, which are gender-related conceptions of themselves and others, and that these schemas influence children's thinking and behavior. Although similar to Kohlberg's theory in the assumption that children play an active role in gender development, gender-schema theory assumes a more basic understanding of gender is all that is required to motivate children's behavior and thinking.
>
> (2004, p. 67)

Thus while Kohlberg's (1966) theory argues that a child's understanding of gender has to be relatively advanced (i.e. the notion of gender constancy) before this knowledge has a significant impact upon behaviour, gender schema theory (Bem, 1981a; Martin & Halverson, 1981) argues that this awareness can be much more simplistic to have an impact upon behaviour. Furthermore the gender schema theory places more emphasis upon the social aspects of cognitions and recognises the cultural specificity of gender schemas and stereotypes.

Further reading

Bem, S. L. (1981). Gender schema theory: A cognitive account of sex typing. *Psychological Review, 88*(4), 354–364.
Martin, C. L. & Halverson, C. F. (1981). A schematic processing model of sex typing and stereotyping in young children. *Child Development, 52*(4), 1119–1134.

Key search terms

Bem Sex Role Inventory (BSRI)
Gender schema theory
Sandra Bem
Schema
Sex typing
Stereotypes

Chapter 9

Social learning theory

In this chapter we will look at social learning theory which presents an alternative proposal for how gender develops during childhood. According to this theory children learn how to be boys or girls following positive or negative reinforcement of behaviours which results in the creation of a gendered identity; thus suggesting that the behaviour precedes the cognition. This theory was first written about with a focus on gender by Mischel (1966) and was heavily influenced by the behaviourist school; however the approach has been popularised and most significantly written about by Bandura (1969, 2003; Bussey & Bandura 1999). In the late 1980s Bandura (1986) suggested that the social learning theory be reformulated as the social cognitive theory, placing emphasis on the cognitive and other internal processes involved; but for simplicity and to avoid confusion with the cognitive theory of gender development, the term social learning theory shall be retained (the social cognitive theory will be explored at the end of the chapter). In the rest of this chapter we will discuss the following:

- Roots of social learning theory: Behaviourism
- Description and evaluation of social learning theory of gender, including the importance of modelling, the processes involved in modelling and the effects of modelling.
- Description and evaluation of social cognitive theory

◉ Roots of social learning theory: Behaviourism

Behaviourism arose in contrast to the psychoanalytic schools of the early twentieth century and proposed an approach to psychology that was not concerned with the internal processes of the mind (such as the id, ego and superego), but was predominantly interested in outwardly measurable behaviour. An analogy that has been used to describe the behaviourist approach is to refer to a clock (Guttenplan, 1994); a behaviourist would be interested in the ticking hands only as that is the outwardly visible marker of time, whereas others (such as psychoanalysts) would be interested in the system beyond the clock face and the mechanisms that drive the clock forward.

In 1913 J. B. Watson published an essay titled 'Psychology as the behaviourist views it' which set forth the key ideas of this new branch of psychology. In this classic essay he argued for a disregarding of psychology's interest in introspection and consciousness, and argued that psychology, as a science of the mind, should attempt to emulate other natural sciences, such as chemistry and physics. He also recommended the use of animals in psychological testing in order to observe measurable behaviour as, from the behaviourist perspective, the consciousness of the organism is not relevant. Watson was particularly interested in the research of Russian physiologist Ivan Pavlov who had conducted studies looking at the conditioned responses of dogs. This was the first paper that argued for a behaviourist approach and it was widely accepted and behaviourism became one of the leading forces in psychology for the first half of the twentieth century. One of the most popular areas of research for behaviourists was the study of **conditioning** (conditioning in this context refers to learning) and behaviourists identified two types of conditioning: classical and operant.

The first type of conditioning is classical conditioning which involves a learned response to a stimulus, that is we learn to associate one object or event with another. This is most famously demonstrated by the work of Pavlov whose research was primarily concerned with the secretion of digestive juices in dogs and the phenomenon of conditioned reflexes (Pavlov was a physiologist, not a psychologist) (Pavlov, 1927). He demonstrated this by conditioning dogs to associate one event with another (most famously a bell associated with food). The second type of conditioning proposed by behaviourists is operant conditioning which was most famously described by B. F. Skinner and this type of learning is based upon rewards and punishments. This was exampled by training rats to associate stimuli with rewards or punishments which led to an altering of behaviour.

Behaviourism has had a long-lasting impact in psychology, such as the use of conditioning in behavioural training and the use of animal studies, but its popularity has waned over the years. This is primarily due to its fundamental dismissal of internal processes and its sole focus on outwardly measurable behaviour. Many approaches to psychology which gained popularity in the latter half of the twentieth century are interested in the internal processes of the mind, whether cognitive processes or neurological structures: no longer is the mind considered a 'black box' of no interest. Thus the cornerstone of behavioural theory proved to be its downfall. However, the focus on learning had a lasting influence and this focus was developed into the social learning theory.

⊙ Social learning theory

In the same volume of work in which Kohlberg's (1966) description of a cognitive approach to gender development appeared, there was also a chapter by Mischel (1966). This was the first contribution towards a social learning theory of gender and its approach was radically different to Kohlberg's. Kohlberg suggested that cognitions take place prior to behaviour, yet Mischel suggested that it is the behaviour that occurs first. If the child behaves in a gender-appropriate manner then they are rewarded and thus the behaviour is reinforced. Thus rather than a child thinking 'I am a boy so I must play in this way' a child might think 'I have been rewarded for playing like a good boy, therefore I must be a boy'. Similarly if a child is punished for behaving in a gender-inappropriate way (such as if a boy is teased for wearing pink), then negative reinforcement occurs and the child avoids this behaviour in future. The similarity between this process and the model of operant conditioning proposed by behaviourists is clear.

The importance of modelling

One aspect of learning that is central to a child's development is the process of modelling (Bandura et al., 1961, 1963; Bussey & Bandura, 1999;

Mischel, 1966; Perry & Bussey, 1979). The importance of modelling is explained below:

> The provision of social models is also an indispensible means of transmitting and modifying behaviour in situations where errors are likely to produce costly or fatal consequences. Indeed, if social learning proceeded exclusively on the basis of rewarding and punishing consequences, most people would never survive the socialization process. Even in some cases where non-social stimuli can be relied upon to elicit some approximation of the desired behaviour, and errors do not result in perilous outcomes, people are customarily spared exceedingly tedious and often haphazard trial-and-error experimentation by emulating the behaviour of socially competent models. In fact, it would be difficult to imagine a socialization process in which the language, mores, vocational and avocational patterns, the familial customs of a culture, and the educational, social, and political practices were shaped in each new member by selective reinforcement without the response guidance of models who exhibit the accumulated cultural repertoires in their own behaviour.
>
> (Bandura, 1969, p. 213)

Put simply, if we only developed via reward/punishment methods of learning then we would be constantly engaged in a trial and error process, but through modelling we can pick up behaviours much quicker, particularly social behaviours that have evolved over time, otherwise we would be continually re-inventing our culture. Thus we learn about the social world and appropriate ways to behave from those around us.

It has been suggested by Bandura (2003) that there are several types of modelling, including verbal, behavioural and symbolic. *Verbal modelling* refers to verbal descriptions of how to behave and act, for example a parent might lay down clear ground rules for appropriate behaviour before the family enter a restaurant. *Behavioural modelling* occurs every day and is perhaps the most basic form of modelling; this is when children learn how to behave by following the lead of the people around them, particularly adults. Bandura (2002a, 2002b) has argued that an increasingly important type of modelling that exists in our current western society is *symbolic*. In our media-saturated society we continuously witness other people's behaviour, whether through the news, through documentaries, films or fictional programmes, and we are even instructed how to act, such as how we are encouraged to vote for a particular political party or to buy

a particular product through advertising. Thus modelling is a varied process and does not simply rely on imitation of those around us. However,
for the developing child this is perhaps the most powerful form of **observational learning** and some of its effects are described in the following
paragraph.

An example of how this learning process might occur is demonstrated
by a well-cited study from 1978 conducted by Fagot who studied the
parent–child interactions of 24 two-parent families. Each of these families had a single child aged between 20 and 24 months and 12 families
had young boys and 12 had young girls; all of the families were white
and came from a middle-class background. The researchers conducted a
series of five one-hour-long observations with the family during which
they observed normal everyday interactions between the parents and
child; the parents were aware of the observation, but were not aware that
gender was a topic of interest. The results of the observations revealed
that the parents responded in the following ways:

- When boys played with blocks parents responded more positively
  than when girls did.
- Girls received more positive comments when they played with dolls
  than when boys did.
- When boys played with dolls and other soft toys their fathers
  responded more negatively than their mothers did.
- When girls engaged in active play (such as running, jumping and
  climbing) they received more negative comments from their parents
  than boys did.
- When the children asked for help, the girls received more positive
  responses and the boys more negative.
- The female toddlers were encouraged to help their parents with
  household chores more than the boys were and received more
  positive comments when they attempted to help.
- The female toddlers were encouraged to remain in close proximity
  to their parents, particularly their fathers.

Thus an interesting set of results appear where the toddlers are encouraged by either positive or negative feedback from parents to behave
in gender stereotypical ways with regard to both play and non-play
behaviours. Boys are encouraged to be independent, to not ask for help
and to play in gender-typical ways (such as with blocks, not dolls), while
the girls are encouraged to be dependent upon their parents, to help

around the house and to play with dolls. So even at a very young age before gender cognitions are considered to be basic (let alone reach the sophisticated level of gender constancy as suggested by Kohlberg (1966)) toddlers are being encouraged to act in gender-appropriate ways and discouraged from behaving in gender-inappropriate ways. This provides evidence for the social learning theory with children being socialised into a gender identity by those around them (particularly their parents), rather than being motivated by their own cognitive processes.

Effects of modelling

However, observational learning does not simply result in mimicry of the modelled behaviour, but it has been suggested that there are four possible effects of modelling in observers (Rosenthal & Bandura, 1978):

1   The first is observational learning effects which result in new behaviours on the part of the observer; this is obviously the optimal result from a modelling encounter. The child witnesses a behaviour which it is able to mimic and add to its own repertoire of activities.

2   The second is referred to as inhibitory and disinhibitory effects; this modelling effect results in the inhibition or encouragement of behaviours that already exist in the child's repertoire. This predominantly occurs based on the consequences of the model's behaviour.

   a.   A modelling behaviour will have an inhibitory effect if it results in the child refraining from that activity, so, for example, a child may perceive negative effects when an adult behaves in a gender-inappropriate way (such as a boy liking ballet) and so refrain from indulging that personality trait in themselves.

   b.   On the other hand a modelling behaviour may result in disinhibitory effects whereby a previously repressed (due to its socially unacceptable nature) behaviour in the child is more often engaged in after witnessing a model receive no negative outcome. A child, for example, may witness an older child being rewarded in some way after misbehaving and so attempts to attain the same rewards by indulging in the same behaviour.

3   The third type of modelling effect is termed response facilitation effects whereby an individual will increase an activity based on the observation of others. This is different from the observational learning effects as it is not a new behaviour that is learnt, nor

does it involve a repressed behaviour as in disinhibitory effects. A pubescent girl may witness, for example, how her peers are using and talking about make-up and so may engage in the same behaviours.

4 The fourth function of modelling effects suggested (Rosenthal & Bandura, 1978) is that the behaviours of models serve as cognitive standards for self-regulation. Thus we integrate the behaviour of others into our own frameworks of what is acceptable behaviour and we might then adapt our frameworks accordingly. We then use these standards to judge our own behaviour.

Thus modelling is not a simple case of mimicry with a child merely imitating the actions of those around them, but have a number of effects which can either encourage or discourage particular actions.

The social learning theory has proved popular over the years and has also been supported by many empirical studies (such as Bandura et al., 1961, 1963; Fagot, 1978). However it has been criticised for not paying sufficient attention to the cognitive elements that contribute towards the development of gender. However, Bandura (1986) has gone some way to address these criticisms by developing the social cognitive theory, to which we will now turn our attention.

👁 Social cognitive theory

This is a modification of the social learning theory (Mischel, 1966) and attempts to place more emphasis of the cognitive aspects of the process (Bandura, 1986). Bandura (1986, 2004) attempted to strengthen the social learning theory by the incorporation of internal processes (particularly cognitions) which is something that was absent from the original theory. He suggested a **triadic reciprocal causation**; this, put more simply, suggests that there are three factors which interrelate with one another and affect our preparedness to learn. The three aspects are behaviour, internal processes (such as cognition, emotion and anticipated outcomes) and the external environment. Bandura (1997) has argued that there are three types of environment:

- IMPOSED
  This is the first kind of environment Bandura lists and this refers to an environment which individuals have no choice but

to experience. Children, for example, do not choose to go to school, but must.

- SELECTED
  This is an environment that we do have some control over. The school, for example, is an imposed environment, but within school children can select their own peer groups and thus select their social environment.
- CREATED
  We also have the ability to create our own environments; children may be able to choose how to decorate their bedroom or decorate their school lockers how they wish. Thus we are able to create some environments in which we operate.

These suggested types of environments place more emphasis on the role of the individual, rather than simply casting the child as a passive element in its own world: the young boy or girl is proposed as being able to actively shape their environment. Furthermore given the four stages of success-ful modelling (discussed earlier) that Bandura (1986) suggested the social cognitive theory places more emphasis on the individual's cognitive abil-ities to master their own environment and behaviour. Thus the social cognitive theory of gender development (Bandura, 1986) does retain some of its focus on the external environment, but places much more empha-sis on the individual's own agency and cognitive processes within that environment.

Processes involved in modelling

So how does modelling take place? One of the criticisms, which you might have noticed yourself, is that the social learning theory does not explain how modelling takes place, just that it takes place. This was one of the approaches main weakness, but this was improved when Bandura (1986) suggested a process as to how observational learning occurs. He proposed that this was a four-step process which will be described below:

1 ATTENTIONAL PROCESSES
   We witness thousands of behaviours everyday – in real life and through the media – but we only pay attention to a relatively small number in terms of observational learning. There are a number of factors which can focus our attention on a particular modelling activity, for example we are more likely to pay attention to same-sex

role models (Bandura et al., 1961, 1963; Bussey & Bandura, 1984). Other factors that influence the attentional processes include the prevalence, complexity and functional value of the modelled behaviour, while the cognitive capability of the child is also likely to have an impact.

2 RETENTION PROCESSES

Once our attention has been focused on a modelling behaviour, that modelling is no good to us unless we remember it and "retention involves an active process of transforming and restructuring information about events for memory representation in the form of rules and conceptions of styles of behaviour" (Bussey & Bandura, 1999, p. 687). It is not enough to simply imitate the modelled behaviours, the child has to cognitively transform the observed behaviour so that it has meaning for them. This stage is particularly reliant upon the child's cognitive capabilities, such as the ability to symbolically recode information and to categorise it.

3 PRODUCTION PROCESSES

Once the child has a symbolic representation of the modelled behaviour it needs to be able to transform understanding into practice, that is it needs to be able to perform the modelled behaviour. Once the child has performed the behaviour it will assess its performance against the original modelled behaviour and may make alterations based on self-feedback.

4 MOTIVATIONAL PROCESSES

The final stage refers to the motivation of the child in performing the behaviours it has learnt as we all learn a multitude of behaviours that we could perform but choose not to. A child will learn, for example, what it means to act like the opposite sex, but chooses not to display those behaviours and maintain gender-appropriate behaviour. It has been shown, for example, that the acquisition of gendered behaviours is the same for both boys and girls, but it is the performance that differs (Bandura, 1965).

An example of how these processes might work and so how modelled behaviours become learnt comes from a study by Dunn et al. (1987) who studied the talk between parents and toddlers regarding emotions and feeling states. In the first part of the study the authors studied 43 families and were particularly interested in the second-born child who was between 18 and 24 months old (21 were boys and 22 were girls) at the time of the study. The study involved observing the children for two, one-hour periods during their normal home routines. They found that around the ages of 18 months it was the mother who made most references to feeling states, but by 24 months the toddler was also commenting on this topic frequently. They also found that mothers tended to talk more about feeling states with girls than with boys which is a finding that has been repeatedly replicated (e.g. Adams et al., 1995; Fivush et al., 2000; Kuebli & Fivush, 1992; Leaper et al., 1998). What was particularly interesting in the 1987 (Dunn et al.) study was that by the age of 24 months female toddlers were demonstrating explicitly more feeling talk than their male counterparts, thus it would seem that the girls had internalised this aspect of being a woman (i.e. reinforcing the cultural stereotype of females being more likely to discuss emotional and feeling states than males). Thus we can see how social learning can occur with regard to gender which supports the notion of social learning theory, particularly as at such a young age the children would not have yet formed cognitive notions of gender as suggested by Kohlberg (1966).

◉ Evaluation of social learning theories

There have been criticisms in the past that the social learning theory (and social cognitive theory) of gender did not sufficiently account for the child's own awareness of their developing gender, but rather portrayed the child as a passive actor in its own development. This criticism was staunched somewhat by an article in which Bandura (2001) describes the role of agency in social cognitive theory; additionally the individual is also positioned as having some control over their environment (Bandura, 1986). Also in a study by Bussey and Bandura (1992) the authors emphasised the role of self-regulation in gender-typed behaviour, as children developed strong cognitive models of gender they required less reinforcement from external sources (such as their parents) and were able to judge their own behaviour. Thus there is some awareness that there is a place for the individual's own agency and self-efficacy in the social learning theory. Another point of debate has been due to the importance that the social learning theory places on modelling with some critics arguing that modelling is not as important in gender development as social learning theorists would have us believe. In a 1974 review of research Maccoby and Jacklin came to the conclusion that parental socialisation did not differ according the gender of the child and "that modeling plays a minor role in the development of sex-typed behaviour" (ibid., p. 300). However, a review of their study (Block, 1976) found their methodology to be flawed and so warned caution in accepting their conclusions. Furthermore research has continued to suggest the importance of modelling in the development of gender (e.g. Bussey & Bandura, 1984).

The strongest criticism of the social learning theory is that, due to the importance it assigns to the environment in the development of gender, it pays insufficient attention to the biological, hormonal and neurological factors of gender. Take for example the famous Bobo doll experiment (Bandura et al., 1961, 1963) which has been seen as a classic experiment that demonstrates the impact of modelling on aggressive behaviour. While environment does have an impact on aggression, it has also been demonstrated that so do biological factors, such as hormones (Archer, 1991; Book et al., 2001; Ramirez, 2002). However, despite its flaws, social learning theory remains a strong research direction in the field of gender development and offers researchers a valid alternative to the gender schema theory (Bem, 1981a; Martin & Halverson, 1981) and cognitive theories of development (Kohlberg, 1966).

◉ Chapter summary

Throughout this chapter we have looked at the social learning theory, particularly as proposed by Bandura (1986, 1997, 2004); and this theory argues that children learn through modelling the behaviours of others. However, this is not a case of simple mimicry, but a case of the child actively adopting or rejecting the behaviours on the basis of how socially successful the modelled behaviours are. Young children are constantly looking to those around them, particularly those in important roles (such as caregivers or peers). Much empirical evidence has been found to support the notion of social learning theory (although there are also some criticisms as descried above) and the theory continues to provide researchers with a plausible explanation for the development of gender.

◉ Further reading

Bussey, K. & Bandura, A. (1999). Social-cognitive theory of gender development and differentiation. *Psychological Review, 106*(4), 676–713.

◉ Key search terms

Albert Bandura
Social cognitive theory
Social learning theory
Triadic reciprocal causation

Chapter 10

Social
constructionism

In this chapter we will address a final area of psychological theory and discuss social constructionism. This is a theoretical standpoint which has increased in popularity since the 1980s and has emerged as a popular replacement to cognitive perspectives. It offers an alternative to cognition- or biology-based theories and emphasises the role of the wider cultural environment upon the behaviours, development and language of the individual. In this chapter we shall discuss the following points:

- Description of social constructionism
- Social constructionism and the development of gender
- Introduction to the work of Lev Vygotsky
- Evaluation of social constructionist approaches to gender

👁 The social constructionist family

Social constructionism has become an increasingly popular approach in recent years, particularly for social psychologists and those who do not subscribe to mainstream cognitive perspectives. It originally began to emerge as a psychological viewpoint in the 1960s and grew out of ethnography and anthropology which considers the cultural aspect of behaviour to be of central importance. In essence social constructionism argues that the cultural and historical specificity of behaviour is key and it is the social environment that constitutes the important aspect to behaviour. However, a definition for social constructionism still remains elusive: it is used as an umbrella term to describe a multitude of researchers, methodologies and theories which can have nothing more in common than a mere family resemblance to each other (Cromby, 2004; Harré, 2002; Potter, 1996; Stam, 2001), with Kenneth Gergen referring to this semblance as a "shared consciousness" (1973, p. 266). In essence the term reflects a general underpinning that human action, knowledge and behaviour are grounded in the social world.

Gergen (1985), one of the leading proponents of social constructionism in psychology, cites four central ideas:

1 A critical assessment of our knowledge, that is a stance that questions mainstream approaches and ideas that are taken for granted by many psychologists.
2 The historical and cultural specificity of knowledge, so the idea that particular understandings exist in a specific culture.
3 The acknowledgement that knowledge is developed, bound up with and created by social processes, for example scientific processes operate in a particular way (such as ways of behaving in a laboratory).
4 That social action and knowledge are entangled, so it is impossible to separate the cultural from the factual.

One of the implications of these ideas is that "there can be no such thing as an objective fact" (Burr, 2003, p. 6) and as such 'truth' is thrown sharply into question. As cultures change over time beliefs, attitudes and 'facts' are altered too, for example the American continent did not exist in European conceptions of the world until Columbus' voyages in the 1490s. With regard to gender it was considered a fact for many centuries that men held dominion over women; this is obviously no longer the case. Thus as our perceptions of the world change, so do our realities and therefore it can be said that there is no objective reality (Gergen, 1973).

One of the principles that unites most constructionist research is that it offers a challenge to mainstream psychology because it refutes the notion that 'facts' can be arrived at by unbiased, independent and impartial investigation of the phenomena in question (Burr, 2003; Cromby, 2004; Gergen, 1985; Harré, 2002; Potter, 1996). Thus researchers are encouraged not to accept knowledge that is taken for granted, but to take a questioning and critical approach. This is in line with the earlier point that there is no such thing as an objective fact; our understanding is constantly shifting and evolving and so it is important to make adjustments to our knowledge based on this. So given recent advancements in understanding of gender dysphoria, transsexualism and genetic disorders, it could be argued that our previous understanding of just two sexes (male and female) is now limited and should be updated (Fausto-Sterling, 1993). Thus social constructionism understands gender as connected to and part of the cultural environment in which we operate our daily lives.

Social and historical specificity of gender development

Given the great importance placed upon the social environment, it is not surprising that one of the central ideas of social constructionism is the focus on cultural and historical specificity. This issue is particularly explored in the final two chapters of this book where we look at contemporary notions of gender around the world and take a look at previous understandings that have existed in the United Kingdom. It is worth making clear at this juncture how these issues relate to the development of gender. In a classic paper from 1973 social psychologist Kenneth Gergen argues for a framing of social psychological knowledge with history as "a concentration on psychology alone provides a distorted understanding of our present condition" (Gergen, 1973, p. 319). In essence he argues for a wider look at the contemporary and historical context of social interactions. Just as it is distorting to look at the financial success of a business without an understanding of the wider political economy or the behaviour of an animal without an understanding of the local ecology, so it is important to locate human behaviour, interactions and activities within a wider cultural context.

With regard to gender development the cultural environment is even more of a salient issue as gender itself is a cultural context (as discussed in the first chapter). Predominant notions of masculinity and femininity will have a significant and lasting impact upon how a child is raised and socialised. Again, these are issues that are explored in detail in the final two chapters, but it is worth giving an illustrative example at this point. In Chapter 11 there is a description of changing laws which have affected women over the last two centuries and they illustrate how 'being' a woman or 'doing' femininity has changed dramatically over this time.

A young woman born in 1800 was not allowed to vote, was not allowed to own property, was not allowed to go to university and even receiving a basic education was a privilege not a right. If her husband treated her poorly she was not entitled to a divorce and in the case of separation she was not entitled to see her children. The thought of a woman choosing a career over marriage was not even conceivable; even Florence Nightingale in the mid-1800s received opposition from her family when she began her nursing career. On the other hand the lives of women have certainly improved and a female born in the year 2000 can expect a very different experience. Nowadays women are entitled to (and receive) the same education as men, are encouraged to attend university, are expected to go into a career of their choosing, to marry from love should they choose to do so and own property in their own right. These differences in cultural expectations have a significant impact upon child-rearing practices:

> ... the type of socialization practices directed toward girls and boys may reflect the existing opportunity structures for women and men in a particular community at a particular time in history. For example, if women are expected to be primarily responsible for raising their children, childhood practices would be more apt to emphasize the practice of nurturant behaviors in girls than in boys. If men are expected to be primarily responsible for economic subsistence outside of the home, childhood practices would be more apt to emphasize the practice of independent behaviors in boys than in girls. Indeed, cross-cultural studies do reveal that the division of labour according to gender is correlated with child rearing practices in societies (e.g. Hewlett, 1991; Weisner, 1979; Whiting, 1986).
>
> (Leaper, 2000, p. 129)

These differences in cultural circumstances will obviously have an important impact upon the way children, both male and female, are raised and so it is sensible to take the wider cultural environment into account when attempting to understand the development of gender in childhood.

⊙ Social constructionism and language

One particular focus for social constructionists is the use of language. Language is perhaps the most culturally and historically specific tool that we have in our repertoire; after all language and society are intricately entwined and language quickly evolves to reflect and enact cultural movements. In the past few years, for example, English has developed to include a range of technological developments, with terms such as 'internet', 'web 2.0' and 'Facebook' now part of our common language, but not existing until relatively recently. In the 1980s an area of study emerged in psychology which turned researchers' attention to language and argued that discourse (either written or spoken) is more reflective of actual everyday activity. It argued against the theorising of researchers based on observation, statistics or cognitive models and rejected the mainstream notion that there are objective structures or entities that form psychological 'objects' such as beliefs, attitudes or theory of mind (e.g. Antaki, 2004); in this view these 'objects' are created, formed and located within interaction. Furthermore the study of language is not simply recognition of its importance in communication but an acknowledgement that it is fundamental to our thought processes (Burr, 1998).

This study of language has remained central to social constructionist investigations and can reveal much about the cultural constructs we operate with and within our daily lives. With regard to gender we can easily see how language is used to reinforce, dispel or subvert cultural notions regarding gender. Even the act of naming a new child is a linguistic act that contributes to the construction of that child's gender: "To name a baby Mary is to do something that makes it easy for a wide range of English speakers to maintain the initial 'girl' attribution" (Eckert & McConnell-Ginet, 2003, p. 15). As children develop they learn to use language in different ways and it has been found that women are more tentative in their language use than men (Carli, 1990), are politer (Hartman, 1976) and are less likely to interrupt (West & Zimmerman, 1983); overall women's use of language is seen to reflect a lower power status while men tend to display more confidence (Eckert & McConnell-Ginet, 2003). It has also been found that linguistic terms themselves reflect cultural notions of gender; for example it has been found that there are many more sexually derogatory terms for women than there are for men (Burr, 1998).

We will now move on to look at the work of Vygotsky whose connection between language and personal thought has proved to be of interest to social constructionists.

Thinking scientifically → **The egg and the sperm**

In a 1991 article Emily Martin examined the language around reproduction in medical textbooks and how it reflects a narrative regarding
romance and stereotypical gender roles. She looked at scientific discourse and revealed the everyday language that cast the egg and the
sperm into typical gender roles. The egg for example is seen as passive
and is 'swept' along the fallopian tubes, whereas the sperm is referred
to as active, stronger and ultimately 'penetrates' the egg. She writes:

*At its extreme, the age-old relationship of the egg and the sperm
takes on a royal or religious patina. The egg coat, its protective bar-
rier, is sometimes called its "vestments," a term usually reserved for
sacred, religious dress. The egg is said to have a "corona," a crown, and
to be accompanied by "attendant cells." It is holy, set apart and above,
the queen to the sperm's king. The egg is also passive, which also
means it must depend upon the sperm for rescue. Gerald Schatten
and Helen Schatten liken the egg's role to that of Sleeping Beauty: "a
dormant bride waiting her mate's magic kiss, which instills the spirit
that brings her to life." Sperm, by contrast, have a "mission," which is
to "move through the female genital tract in quest of the ovum." One
popular account has it that the sperm carry out a "perilous journey"
into the "warm darkness," where some fall away "exhausted." "Sur-
vivors" "assault" the egg, the successful candidates "surrounding the
prize." Part of the urgency of this journey, in more scientific terms,
is that "once released from the supportive environment of the ovary,
an egg will die within hours unless rescued by a sperm." The word-
ing stresses the fragility and dependency of the egg, even though the
same text acknowledges elsewhere that sperm also live for only a few
hours. (Martin, 1991, p. 490)*

Thus we can see how even the seemingly scientific language of
textbooks used by medical students is imbued with language that
reinforces cultural notions of gender.

Lev Vygotsky

Vygotsky provides a persuasive account of how thought and language
are socialised in the classic text *Thought and Language* (1986). Within
it he argues that children learn about the world through interaction, in
particular that conversations become socialised into the child's internal
thought processes. This is not just limited to verbal activity, but also

through the reciprocity and conversational rhythms that exist in early infancy; for example when infants coo and gurgle, sensitive caregivers respond to these noises as if an actual conversation is occurring and so patterns become embedded in interpersonal processes. These conversational practices then become 'self-talk' as the child continues to negotiate the complexities of language (such as the constant narrative speech of a toddler) and as these intricacies of speech are overcome the verbal nature of language is internalised and becomes thought. It is useful to consider this a model for how emotions also become socialised as demonstrated in the quote below:

> One needs to know how to get emotional properly by expressing it in public before one ever gets to the stage of experiencing a private emotion and holding it back. Similarly, it is clear that people only learn how to talk to themselves on the basis of their experience of actual interpersonal conversation (cf. Vygotsky, 1986).
>
> (Parkinson, 1995, p. 279)

Shame and pride, for example, have been shown to exist only in the presence of other individuals, before they develop within the child. Specifically, notions of shame and pride relied upon the shame and pride of others, and it is only later that children were able to feel shame and pride by themselves (Harter & Whitesell, 1989). This is in keeping with Vygotsky's (1986) account of how children first have to have an experience socially before it can be internalised. This reinforces Vygotsky's statement that:

> Every function in the child's cultural development appears twice: first, on the social level, and later, in the individual level; first, between people (interpsychological) and then inside the child (intrapsychological) ... All the higher functions originate as actual relationships between individuals.
>
> (1978, p. 57)

These processes of internalisation however are managed and mediated by environmental and material resources, such as the caregiver's verbal ability and familial levels of emotional expression; thus if a child is raised in a house where a range of emotions are frequently talked about then the inter- and intra-psychological processes will be more sophisticated than in a child from a house where emotion is not a topic of conversation. Dunn et al. (1987), for example, found that female toddlers were exposed to more talk about emotions than male toddlers, and that those females then spoke more of emotions: the more a toddler was exposed to talk of emotion, the greater the level of internalisation and personalisation. Thus through conversation female toddlers are socialised into being more emotional than their male counterparts which is in keeping with wider cultural notions of gender and the "... child internalizes culture though her or his transactions with other people" (Leaper, 2000, p. 136). Thus we can see by looking at the example of emotion how young children are taught to 'do' gender; in this case that women display more emotion than men.

Social constructionism and gender development

Weisner (1996) argues that it is the cultural environment which has the single greatest influence upon a child's life course, not wealth, not attachment, not education, but society. If one imagines a newborn baby it is easy to understand how such a statement can be made. A baby born and then moved to another family, a different culture or a new continent would have a very different life path depending upon where they ended up. A female child born in China, but adopted in America or the United Kingdom would have an altered life outcome to a female child left in China, just as a child conceived and born in the United Kingdom, but raised in Pakistan. This is not to claim as Locke did that a new born is a blank slate, but to state that culture has a significant and lasting impact upon a child's life course.

Social constructionist psychology differs on the point of essentialism (which much of mainstream psychology sanctions) which states that there is "some pre-given 'content' to the person" (Burr, 2003, p. 6); social constructionists on the other hand believe that the person is defined by social processes and activities. An attitude or a belief, for example, is not something that exists 'in' the individual, but is something that is created through talk and action; one is not sexist, but displays sexism. Thus "gender is something that people 'do' rather than an aspect of individuals' personalities or predispositions" (Leaper, 2000, p. 127). The extract below from Lorber (1994) eloquently explains how gender is 'done':

> Today, on the subway, I saw a well-dressed man with a year-old child in a stroller. Yesterday, on a bus, I saw a man with a tiny baby in a carrier on his chest. Seeing men taking care of small children in public is

increasingly common – at least in New York City. But both men were quite obviously stared at – and smiled at, approvingly. Everyone was doing gender – the men who were changing the role of fathers and the other passengers, who were applauding them silently. But there was more gendering going on that probably fewer people noticed. The baby was wearing a white crocheted cap and white clothes. You couldn't tell if it was a boy or a girl. The child in the stroller was wearing a dark blue T-shirt and dark print pants. As they started to leave the train, the father put a Yankee baseball cap on the child's head. Ah, a boy, I thought. Then I noticed the gleam of tiny earrings in the child's ears, and as they got off, I saw the little flowered sneakers and lace-trimmed socks. Not a boy after all. Gender done.

(p. 54)

Thinking scientifically → **Nurturing gender**

In a 1973 study reporting field work conducted with the Luo tribe of Kenya, Ember describes how the division of labour tasks around the home can be used to draw conclusions regarding the development and socialisation of gender. It was found that Luo girls tended to display more altruistic and prosocial behaviour, whereas the boys were more likely to display aggression, egotism and dominance. The author describes how between the ages of five and seven girls spend approximately half of their time involved in chores, whereas boys spend around 15 per cent of their time. Chores are divided into feminine or masculine tasks and allocated according to gender, but unfortunately the vast majority of chores are considered to be feminine rather than masculine. The only reason a boy may be assigned a 'feminine' task is if they are a younger sibling and there is lack of daughters in the family. It was found that those boys who engaged in feminine tasks inside the home were much more likely to display feminine behaviour as described above. This is tentatively connected by the author to the nature of tasks the boy is engaged in and the type of behaviours those tasks encourage, such as tending to younger siblings is likely to lead to the socialisation of nurturant behaviour. Thus from this study one can see how the gender division of tasks is not a simple case of chore completion, but is associated with the socialisation and development of certain emotional and behavioural traits.

Thus gender is not automatically given, but is achieved through the use of our bodies, our clothing, our language and our interactions. In the example above the lace trim on the baby's socks works to achieve the social category of 'girl'; certainly it achieves more than any unseen anatomical features might.

One example where it is clear to see how social notions of gender have impacted upon development is research regarding the emotion of fear. Since the early beginnings of fear research over a century ago it has been consistently found that girls appear to have more fears than boys. Girls have been found to be more afraid of the dark, being kidnapped or killed, of animals and dirt, while boys have reported higher fears for bodily injury, school failure and nightmares; furthermore these fears have been reported to be more intense for girls than boys (Gullone, 2000). It is argued that in self-report measures (which fear investigations tend to utilise) men artificially deflate the number and severity of fears they experience. In a 1992 (Pierce & Kirkpatrick) study, for example, researchers conducted a 72-list-item fear questionnaire with male and female undergraduate students. One month later the students were shown a video with scenes of objects on the questionnaire (such as mice and a rollercoaster ride) and their heart rate was monitored; the students were advised that heart rate is often used as part of lie detector tests. The students were then administered a second questionnaire and it was found that on the re-test the male students scored higher on their fear ratings, while the female scores did not significantly differ between test and re-test. This indicates that the males had artificially (whether consciously or otherwise) lowered their initial questionnaire responses. These results are in line with long-held notions of western masculinity and femininity, as men are socialised to maintain the stereotype of invincibility and female vulnerability is constructed as more socially acceptable with girls socialised to consider their bodies as fragile (Young, 1980). These consistent findings in gender differences indicate the central role of cultural influence in the development of fear. This demonstrates that fear is not a purely biological response, but occurs within a specific social setting: thus we can understand how aspects of personality develop according to cultural notions of gender.

Evaluation of social constructionism

There is an issue with the theorising of Vygotsky unfortunately, which is that he splits the social from the biological as he makes a distinction between "direct, innate, natural forms" and "mediated, artificial mental functions that develop in the process of cultural development" (Vygotsky, 1998, p. 168). This undermines the biological and neurological aspects of gender (and other experiences) which, as described in the second chapter, are an essential aspect; one ultimately cannot have a gender without having a sex. The "cultural development" Vygotsky (ibid.) refers to is enabled and mediated by biology and as Cromby writes: "The embodied gets constitutively enrolled within the social at the same time as it reflexively enables it" (2007, p. 109–110); that is one cannot talk or 'do' gender without having a voice or a body to do it with. Consequently it is essential that the social and the biological are not separated, but acknowledged and subsequently treated as intertwined, but this remains something of an on-going weakness with social constructionist approaches.

There is also a lack of description as to how these socialisation processes take place. Russell (1989) makes an attempt to describe how emotions are internalised, but there is yet a detailed attempt to theorise how gender is socialised and personalised. In his 2000 review of the development of gender Leaper draws in particular upon social learning theory and modelling (as described earlier) to describe how this might take place, but does not address why the social constructionist approach to gender development is therefore different compared to the social learning theory of gender development.

◉ Chapter summary

In this chapter we have briefly explored social constructionism and the implications of this approach for gender studies. This theoretical stance posits the social and historical specificity of an activity or behaviour as central and argues that gender (or any other psychological phenomenon) is not a predetermined entity, but something that is done and achieved through actions, belongings and language; in an earlier example from Lorber (1994), for example, we saw how the gender construct of 'girl' was achieved through the lace trim on a pair of socks. We explored language in particular as a cultural tool which is often invoked and used in a variety of ways to achieve constructed phenomena and as such is of particular interest to researchers working in this field. We also looked at the work of Vygotksy who described how the social becomes the personal. While social constructionism offers a popular alternative to mainstream psychological theories, it has been as yet unfortunately unsuccessful in offering a comprehensive account of how these processes of socialisation take place, and this remains a flaw for those interested in developmental processes. However, the social constructionist focus on cultural and historical specificity will be explored in the next two chapters.

Further reading

Leaper, C. (2000). The social construction and socialization of gender during development. In P. H. Miller and E. K. Scholnick (Eds), *Towards a feminist developmental psychology* (pp. 127–152). New York and London: Routledge.

Key search terms

Discourse analysis
Kenneth Gergen
Linguistic turn
Social constructionism
Lev Vygotsky

Chapter 11

History of gender

In this chapter we will explore how concepts of gender have changed in our culture. While we now live in a culture that promotes equality for the genders this has not always been the case and, if we are to fully understand what it means to grow up as a boy and a girl in contemporary Britain, it is important to understand what it has meant to be male and female in the past. While it is impossible to provide a detailed history of gender in the United Kingdom in a few thousand words, this chapter will aim to historically map out how notions of masculinity and femininity have changed. We will also look at some events – such as the suffrage movement – in particular detail as they represent key points that have shaped our current idea of gender. In the following pages we will address the following:

- Adam and Eve
- Suffrage movement
- The feminist movements

👁 Adam and Eve

This may seem like a step too far back to begin our historical look at gender, but it is the starting point for our contemporary notions of masculinity and femininity and so is worthy of exploration. Western culture is based upon Christianity and although secularism may be on the rise in Britain and although we may live in a multi-faith society, we fundamentally live according to Christian guidelines and our notions of gender are based upon biblical representations of the sexes. While it may seem biased to focus solely on Judeo-Christian heritage the focus of this book has been on western societies and these cultures, while steeped in the rich diversity of a contemporary multi-cultural way of life, are founded on a Judeo-Christian religion.

In order to understand these representations it is necessary to start at the beginning in the Garden of Eden. The Christian tale of creation, as told in Genesis, recounts that God made the heavens, earth and all its creatures in six days (God rested on the seventh day). Adam was created so that he could tend to the new world God had completed and was created from the earth he was to guard: "the Lord God formed the man from the dust of the ground and breathed into his nostrils the breath of life, and the man became a living being" (Genesis 2: 7, New International Version). And so Adam was born from the earth and without a companion, however "the Lord God said, 'It is not good for the man to be alone. I will make a helper suitable for him'" (Genesis, 2: 18). Thus Eve was made to be a helper, rather than an equal companion from the very beginning. God placed Adam into a deep sleep and removed one of his ribs, from which he created Eve and so woman was created from man. Eve, from the outset, is therefore conceptualised as Adam's inferior being: he is her creator and master, she just his helper. It was, however, the tale of the Fall which sealed Eve's fate as a subordinate, even though Adam was present with Eve when she first ate the forbidden fruit. Furthermore her punishment (and that of womankind in general) was that her husband "will rule over" (Genesis, 3: 16) her, thus her position as a subordinate is confirmed and described as an eternal punishment.

The roles of Adam and Eve have shaped our understanding of gender for centuries; Eve was created for and from Adam and so was his subordinate and she was also interpreted as the cause of the original sin. For centuries after the myth the role of Eve has been transformed into a cause for the subjugation of women, a tale that is reinforced by the Bible itself as Crowther writes:

> For many exegetes, Eve's role in the Fall was clear proof that women were more gullible, less rational, and more prone to evil than men. All women, like their mother Eve, were potentially dangerous and disorderly. Paul exemplifies this view of Eve and this attitude toward women. In his first letter to Timothy, he declared,
>
> I suffer not a woman to teach, nor to usurp authority over the man, but to be in silence. For Adam was first formed, then Eve. And

Adam was not deceived, but the woman being deceived was in the transgression.

(Timothy 2: 12–14)

Thus the threat posed by women could only be contained if they were firmly under the control of male authorities.

(2010, p. 99)

We can also witness how women are literally invisible in the biblical family tree:

When Adam had lived 130 years, he had a son in his own likeness, in his own image; and he named him Seth. After Seth was born, Adam lived 800 years and had other sons and daughters. Altogether, Adam lived 930 years, and then he died.

When Seth had lived 105 years, he became the father of Enosh. And after he became the father of Enosh, Seth lived 807 years and had other sons and daughters. Altogether, Seth lived 912 years, and then he died.

When Enosh had lived 90 years, he became the father of Kenan. And after he became the father of Kenan, Enosh lived 815 years and had other sons and daughters. Altogether Enosh lived 905 years, and then he died.

When Kenan had lived 70 years, he became the father of Mahalalel. And after he became the father of Mahahlalel, Kenan lived 840 years and had other sons and daughters. Altogether Kenan lived 910 years, and then he died.

(Genesis, 5:3–15)

This continues for several generations until we are introduced to Noah (who rescued God's creatures from flood waters). What is noticeably absent from this family line is women; no mothers, wives or sisters are mentioned by name and so it appears as if the sons were created by their fathers without the aid of women. It also conceptualises the Christian family as patrilineal with only the eldest sons mentioned by name. And so the Christian story of Adam, Eve and their descendants – the first family according to the bible – establishes the role of the woman as subordinate and patriarchy as the ruling structure.

Furthermore the portrayal of women in the bible focuses predominantly on their birthing capabilities; Eve after all was created to be a companion and a mate for Adam. This procreational role for women is emphasised by God from the very beginning of humankind:

> At the same time, the story of the creation of Eve was often taken to indicate that God intended most humans to marry and produce children. Just as God had not wanted Adam to be alone and had created a companion for him, so marriage was the natural state of the first couple's descendants . . . God's words to Adam and Eve – 'increase and multiply' – were part of the marriage ceremony from the early centuries of Christianity.
>
> (Crowther, 2010, p. 99)

Thus another role is assigned to women – that of child bearer. This acts to reinforce patriarchal notions of progeny and domesticity where the male roles are played outside of the home, while the female roles lie within it.

There is a paradox present in Christian and patriarchal mythology which not only presents women as the source of the original sin, but also as the epitome of innocence. This paradox is known as the Madonna/Whore complex whereby women are conceptualised of in terms of a dichotomy; either they are whores or virgins. Eve falls within the 'whore' category as she was a woman who did not do as man (or God) instructed her to and consequently had to be punished. Madonna represents the ultimate virgin and the ultimate mother figure; she was the mother of the saviour of mankind according to Christian lore, but also retained her innocence and virginity. Thus while women are praised and celebrated for their child-bearing capabilities, it is not in keeping with the Madonna conceptualisation for women to express a desire for or knowledge of sexual matters, and if desire is shown then the woman risks being associated with promiscuity.

These Christian and patriarchal ideas shaped our notions of gender for many centuries; they tied women to the roles of wife and mother while allowing men to master the world. There were of course notable exceptions to this rule – such as Queen Elizabeth I – but they were special cases, were very clearly operating in a man's world and were living at the very edges of culturally acceptable femininity. And so the status quo was woman as servant to her husband, father and son and man as ruler of all until relatively recently when concepts of gender began to radically change.

👁 The suffrage movement

In this section we shall explore how universal suffrage was achieved, from both the male and female perspectives. It is often taken for granted that it is the female franchise that is the most important tale to tell, but the male fight for equal franchise was just as arduous and it was a long time before the political opinions of the lower classes were considered worthy of the vote.

👁 The male vote

While the majority of texts regarding the suffrage movement focus on the fight for the female vote, it is important to remember that there was also a male suffrage movement. The fight for the male vote in the United Kingdom is more a story of class than of gender and represents how gender is not the only factor in equality, but how social class is often a greater determinant of progress. While there is something of a scarcity of literature in this area (i.e. compared to the academic writings regarding the female suffrage movement), it is possible to track the male franchise through the passing of relevant Bills and Acts of Parliament.

At the beginning of the nineteenth century just 3 per cent of the adult population in Britain was eligible to vote, with the remaining 97 per cent excluded as they held insufficient property; in order to vote, put simply, you had to be wealthy. This changed in 1832 with the first Reform Act which extended the vote to those who held lands worth £10 per annum. While this was a step in the right direction it was a tiny step as this was still a vast sum of money in those days; the 1832 Act still excluded six out of seven adult males from political representation. In 1867 the Second Reform Act extended the property requirements again, particularly in the urban areas, and effectively doubled the voting population from one to two million (the population of the United Kingdom at that time was approximately 30 million). Finally the Third Reform Act (1884) established an equal franchise in both rural and urban areas, but there were still millions of men (approximately 40 per cent of adult males) who were unable to vote as they did not meet the property requirements. Although the boundary had dropped considerably, a man still had to rent or buy a certain amount of property in order to vote and this meant that majority of the adult population in the United Kingdom still had no political representation. It was not until 1918 that all men over 21, regardless of property ownership or wealth, were given the vote which was in recognition of the great sacrifices displayed by men (particularly working class men) during First World War.

Thus the history of male suffrage is more a tale of class than of gender. The upper classes were the dominant force in Britain for many centuries and it was not until the industrialisation and urbanisation of the Victorian era that this began to change. Finally it was not until millions of young men lost their lives on the muddy fields of the Great War that all men were awarded the right to vote regardless of wealth.

The female vote

The female suffrage movement took off after the 1867 Reform Act; there had been a section in the Bill put forward by John Stuart Mill that proposed giving the vote to women, but this part of the Bill was overwhelmingly defeated. After this defeat the female suffrage movement began to spread and many small groups sprang up in support of female franchise. These groups were relatively unsuccessful and operated on a small scale until they were united in 1897 by the founding of the NUWSS (National Union of Women's Suffrage Societies). The NUWSS was run by Millicent Fawcett (after the death of the first President Lydia Decker) and was firmly committed to non-violent means of political reformation. It organised the local branches whilst they conducted marches, peaceful demonstrations, gave talks, wrote letter to politicians and distributed literature to the press and the public.

However, the peaceful protestations of the NUWSS were felt to be too passive by some, particularly by the Pankhursts (Emmeline and her daughters Christabel and Sylvia):

> When Christabel said to her mother one day in 1903, 'It is unendurable to think of another generation of women wasting their lives begging for the vote ... We must act', Emmeline took note. 'After that', she recollected, 'I and my daughters together sought a way to bring about that union of young and old which would find new methods, blaze new trails.' Thus on 10 October 1903, together with a small group of socialist women suffragists, she founded the WSPU, to campaign for the parliamentary vote for women on the same terms as it is, or shall be, granted to men. As Emmeline recollected,

'We resolved to limit our membership exclusively to women . . . and to be satisfied with nothing but action on our question. Deeds, not words, was to be our permanent motto'.

(Purvis, 2011, p. 98)

Therefore the Women's Social and Political Union (WSPU) was founded in 1903 by Emmeline and Christabel Pankhurst; the party believed in much more direct action and, although much smaller than the NUWSS, their members took the fight for universal suffrage to the next level with their motto 'Deeds Not Words'. In time the WSPU members became known as 'suffragettes' and also became known for their often illegal ways of campaigning; they broke windows, chained themselves to fences, were involved in violent altercations with the police and were often imprisoned for their activities. Once in prison the more dedicated suffragettes went on hunger and thirst strike which was first carried out by Marion Wallace-Dunlop who wished to be acknowledged as a political (rather than a criminal) prisoner; she fasted for 91 hours and was released as the authorities did not wish to make her a martyr. The tactic was adopted by many other suffrage prisoners and the government responded by allowing controversial force-feeding. Eventually in 1913 the government passed the Prisoner's Temporary Discharge of Ill Health in 1913 which became known as the Cat and Mouse Act; once a prisoner became ill from hunger strike they were released, allowed to return to health and then returned to prison to complete their sentence. Emmeline Pankhurst herself was imprisoned 13 times and went on both hunger and thirst strikes (although she was never force fed) (Purvis, 2011), while Sylvia was force fed during one of her imprisonments (Purvis, 2008).

In 1914 when World War I was declared the NUWSS and WSPU both called a halt to their campaign activities and encouraged their members to show patriotism and support the war effort. The efforts made by women during the 1914–1918 war proved to be the suffrage supporters' most glorious role yet and they were duly awarded the vote in 1917. However the Qualification of Women Act did not provide equal suffrage: it allowed women the vote if they were over the age of 30 as long as they were householders, married to householders, rented a house worth more than £5 a year or had a university education; in the same year it also became legal for women to stand for Parliament as MPs. It was not until the Universal Franchise Act of 1928 that the vote was granted on equal terms to men and women, that is all men and all women over the age of 21 were eligible to vote. In 1969 the voting age was lowered, for both men and women, to 18 under the Representation of the People Act.

Thinking scientifically → **The legal rights of women**

One way in which a society's conceptualisation of gender can be examined is through its laws. There used to be a legal concept called 'coverture' which "upon marriage deprived a woman of her independent legal existence" (Shanley, 1986, p. 72) and in essence a married couple was considered to be one person and that person was the husband. Any property belonging to the woman was automatically transferred to the ownership of her husband, both property owned before marriage and property inherited during the union. Coverture was also used as a reason to deny the female franchise as it was believed that the husband's vote was considered sufficient for both members of the marriage. Thankfully the legal system has made considerable progress in terms of gender equality and major milestones of the British legal system can be seen below:

- In 1839 the Custody of Infants Act meant that mothers were able to apply for custody for children under the age of seven. The Lord Chancellor himself had to agree to the custody and would only allow it if the mother was of upstanding character and had not been accused of adultery.
- In 1857 the Matrimonial Causes Act made it possible to divorce without appealing to Parliament. Prior to this it was possible to divorce, but only if an Act of Parliament was granted which made it very expensive. After 1857 it was possible for a husband to divorce his wife on the grounds of adultery, however a woman could not divorce her husband for the same reason but had to also cite another reason (such as abandonment, rape or extreme cruelty). Up until 1857 it was also still legal for a man to lay claim to the property or earnings of his wife, even after he had divorced her.
- In 1872 the Married Women's Property Act was passed in the United Kingdom which represented a major milestone in the legal rights of women. It stated that any property inherited or money earned by the woman could be retained by her and did not automatically become her husband's property.
- The Infant Custody Act of 1873 was ground breaking in that it allowed custody of the child to be decided according to the best

interests of the child, rather than the interests or rights of the parents. The Act also allowed mothers to apply for custody of children who were under the age of 16.

- In 1878 some protection was offered to women who were the victims of domestic abuse. They were able to apply for a protection order and obtain custody of their children.
- In 1880 a second Married Women's Property Act was enacted which corrected some of the loopholes left by the 1872 Act. Most importantly it meant that property owned by women before marriage did not automatically pass over to her husband upon marriage.
- In 1893 a third Married Women's Property Act was passed which gave women legal control of any property they owned, both acquired before and during marriage.
- In 1919 Parliament passed the Sex Disqualification Removal Act which made it illegal to bar women from certain professions, such as legal careers; up to this point a woman could complete a law degree, but was unable to practice (as was the case for Christabel Pankhurst).
- In 1923 it became possible for women to divorce men on the same grounds.
- In 1926 women were given legal rights to buy and sell property in the same way as men

◉ Feminist movement

The stages of feminist progress are worth exploring here as obviously the fight for female equality did not end when women were granted the franchise. There has since been an on-going battle to ensure gender equality in all avenues of life. We will discuss this movement in terms of the feminist movement as this provides a coherent structure for us to follow as we explore how the fight has changed over the decades.

◉ First-wave feminism

The first-wave of feminism (although this term was not used at the time) was concerned with the property and voting rights. Predominantly led by middle-class women (who did not have to work and thus had the time to devote to the cause) supporters fought for the right to vote and the rights of married women (which are explored earlier in this chapter).

👁 Second-wave feminism

The second-wave of feminism is probably the most well-known and took place in the 1960s and 1970s. The women partaking in this movement were campaigning for equality in the home, the workplace and the legal system. This development was part of a much larger civil rights movement which grew out of a very particular social context in America. The civil rights movement began in the 1950s, led by Martin Luther King and colleagues, and suggested a different way of life; one where the white man was not master. The Vietnam War also inspired protests which were further fuelled by the political activism of the 1960s. A new generation was coming to terms with the post-WWII world and was determined to make it a better place for all. Led by a few women in particular, such as Gloria Steinem and Alice Walker, women began to loudly object to the gender equality in the home and the workplace and vowed to make a difference. Women were confined to the home in their role as wife or mother and if they did venture into the workplace then the gender inequality was inescapable. The second-wave feminists fought for equal pay for the genders and to get women in the boardrooms and into traditionally masculine roles; for example, in 1974 26.9 per cent of doctors qualifying were women, in 1983 this rose to 38.1 per cent and in 1993 had risen again to 46.7 per cent (Lambert et al., 1998). Thus there was an increasing awareness that women were able to choose a life outside of domestic roles and could take on jobs that had been traditionally masculine domains.

One important invention that supported the second wave was the invention of the contraceptive pill in the 1960s. Within 5 years of its approval 40 per cent of young married women were using 'the pill' (Goldin & Katz, 2000) demonstrating just how popular and widespread the contraception was. For the first time women could engage in sexual relationships (whether married or otherwise) and did not have to worry about the risk of pregnancy; they were able to take charge of their own fertility. This meant that they were increasingly able to carve out a career for themselves and choose when to have children. This was a crucial step in the women's movement and allowed women like never before to take control of their lives and the role of the pill in the changing status of women in the twentieth century should not be overlooked (Goldin & Katz, 2000).

Third-wave feminism

While the second wave was much more egalitarian than the first movement, it too has been criticised for placing too much attention on the experience of white middle class women. The third wave of feminism began in the early 1990s and is associated with a move towards celebrating choice for women and a focus on women with a variety of ethnic backgrounds and sexualities. The rights of ethnic and lesbian women have been at the fore of this movement, with their experiences finally given the significance they deserve. While the second wave of feminism fought overt forms of sexism, the third wave has been about challenging more subversive ideas regarding what it means to be a woman, such as promoting the rights of lesbian women. It has also sought to unite women across new technologies and has embraced the use of the media and the internet in campaigning for women's rights, particularly the rights of ethnic, lesbian and more impoverished women. The third wave is often seen as fractious with many different movements, but this is also seen to be a recognition of the pluralism of femininities that are now available to the younger generation of women: being a woman in the twenty-first century means whatever the individual woman wants it to mean.

Chapter summary

In this chapter we have witnessed how being male and female, with a particular focus on women, has changed in the United Kingdom over the years. We started with a look at Christianity and its conceptualisation of women and men which began with the first man and woman: Adam and Eve. Patriarchal interpretations of Christianity meant that for centuries women were cast into the subservient role, with their husbands and fathers in a domineering role. Women were predominantly seen as child-bearers and domestic creatures; they were just wives, mothers and daughters. It was not until the late nineteenth century that this began to change with the suffrage movement and the fight for equality in the legal system. The property, divorce and franchise rights of women meant that progress towards equality was made slowly but surely. The second wave of feminism in the 1960s and 1970s furthered the equality that had been fought for and women were able to create roles for themselves that were no longer limited to the home. Finally the third wave of feminism has shown that the ideal feminine form is not the middle-class white woman, but that being a woman means a whole range of ethnicities, religions, sexualities and classes. The focus in this chapter has been on women, simply because it is the role of women that has undergone the most change in the last century or so.

◉ Further reading

Gillis, S., Howie, G. & Munford, R. (2004). *Third wave feminism: A critical exploration.* Basingstoke, Hampshire: Palgrave Macmillan.

Purvis, J. (2011). Emmeline Pankhurst (1858–1928), suffragette leader and single parent in Edwardian Britain. *Women's History Review, 20*(1), 87–108.

◉ Key search terms

Adam and Eve
Christabel Pankhurst
Emmeline Pankhurst
First-wave feminism
Gender and the bible
Married Women's Property Acts
Second-wave feminism
Suffrage movement
Sylvie Pankhurst
Reform Acts
Third-wave feminism

Chapter 12

Culture and gender

The bulk of the literature referred to in this book was written from a western perspective and therefore with a western notion of gender in mind. However, the west (predominantly America and the United Kingdom in terms of where the majority of academic research comes from) represents just a small proportion of the global population. It is important therefore that we have an understanding of how gender is conceptualised in other cultures and what being male and female means to that particular culture, both to appreciate other societies and to better understand ourselves.

There is not nearly enough room available to do this topic the justice it deserves and so we are limited to the briefest of explorations of gender and gender development in the following areas:

- India – we will look at India due to the clear son preference that has led to a generation of 'missing girls'.
- Africa – while it would be impossible to look at notions of gender in each of Africa's nations we will look at two issues that greatly affect the entire continent, female genital mutilation and the HIV/AIDS crisis.
- Mosou, China – finally we will look at Mosou which represents an alternative society as it is close to a matriarchal society which is virtually non-existent in the rest of the world.

◉ India

The preference for sons in India has long been of media and academic interest; what may be surprising is that the problem has been worsening in recent decades, rather than improving as India seeks to establish itself as a global industrial force. In recent decades the number of girls in India comparable to boys has continued to fall, both due to selective abortions and the relative neglect of female children. In 1981 there were 962 girls (up to the age of 6) for every 1000 boys, in 1991 this fell to 945 girls per 1000 boys and in 2001 this declined again to 927 girls per 1000 boys (Jha et al., 2006). According to Indian law it is illegal to obtain an abortion based solely on the sex of the foetus and it is also prohibited to use ultrasounds and other in-utero tests (such as amniocentesis) to determine the sex of the baby; if the sex is determined accidentally by medical staff then it is against the law for the parents to be informed (Arnold et al., 2002). However, this law does not apply to private institutes and so if they want parents are able to determine the sex of the infant and are also able to obtain an abortion through a private practice, through dangerous illegal abortionists or through self-induced measures. It has been suggested that around 11 per cent of pregnancies in India end due to spontaneous or induced abortion; furthermore with the number of spontaneous abortions rising in recent years (despite improvements in healthcare) researchers have suggested that the cause of these miscarriages is not biological (perhaps deliberately induced or reported as spontaneous when in fact are induced) (Arnold et al., 2002). It is also noteworthy that the sex ratio of children of mothers who have not had an ultrasound or amniocentesis is 107 girls per 100 boys (which is actually higher than the global average of 103–106 girls per 100 boys) (Arnold et al., 2002), thus giving some indication of what the natural sex ratio of Indian infants would be.

The following quotes are taken from a study (Ganatra et al., 2001) in a rural area of India which interviewed over 100 women following an induced abortion, and the extracts demonstrate the pressures and factors leading to the termination of a pregnancy based on sex preference:

> My mother-in-law used to say: 'I won't say anything, but tomorrow if my son starts feeling that he should have a son and if he thinks about remarrying, then don't blame me at that time. You manage

with that'. After all such things, I am having fear in my mind, so I thought let's try and go for checking (the sex).

(p. 115)

The hope for a son was so much that I didn't have any other feeling. I felt sad, but what to do?... There are two daughters, what to do with a third daughter? Nothing else, a son is wanted. Only that is in my mind.

(p. 120)

We have two daughters. We had already decided to... have an operation. I had gone to the hospital. The doctor there said: 'You check it (the sex) first. Why should you go for it (the abortion) if it is a boy!'

(p. 116)

These comments demonstrate that there is a pervasive encouragement to terminate female foetuses, with husbands, relatives, the women themselves and even medical staff reported as considering unborn daughters undesirable.

Not only is infant mortality particularly high among females, but older girls suffer from the general bias towards males; nearly 9 per cent fewer girls receive childhood vaccinations and 6 per cent more girls suffer severe growth stunting due to malnutrition (Pande, 2003). The disadvantage of girls in terms of nutrition and vaccination status is strongly correlated to the literacy of mothers; if mothers are literate then there is no gender gap in treatment of children, but if the mother is illiterate then the girls are likely to fare much worse (Borooah, 2004). Interestingly the role of literacy in the father plays no role, which reinforces the importance of mothers' literacy in relation to child health (Borooah, 2004; DeWalt et al., 2004; Sandiford et al., 1995). Thus the education of women should be a target for government and charity interventions.

This negative attitude towards young females continues into their adult life; in a recent study which involved young men (aged 18–29) researchers reported gender attitudes which demonstrate how women are viewed as inferior to men and as sexual objects:

But aggression to prove manhood was also directed at women – wives, girlfriends and acquaintances. Informants often referred to women as *chhav*, an object or item to be possessed by men. Sexually coercive behaviour was commonly used by men to demonstrate sexual power, including derogatory comments, whistling, jostling, touching and harassment in public places. Sexually coercive activities also included forced kissing and forced intercourse. Very often coercion was directed at women or girls who seemed to challenge masculinity.

(Verma et al., 2006, p. 137)

An aspect of Indian culture that has an impact upon the status of adult women is the maintenance of the caste system. This is a system of social class which is related to Hinduism, but which has evolved beyond the religion and there are five castes which are arranged hierarchically in the following order: Brahman (highest), Kshatriya, Vaishya, Shudra and Harijans (lowest and formerly known as the 'untouchables'). In India the caste of one's family is crucial to social standing and therefore it is important to marry within castes, and due to the importance of the caste system in marriage the traditional practice of dowries remains strong in India and in fact is a flourishing practice and looks set to continue while the caste system remains in practice (Anderson, 2003). What this means for women is that they are literally conceptualised as objects to be bought and sold. Violence towards women is also associated with dowry payments as the following quote demonstrates:

We will illustrate this link with a brief outline of the case of Sannamma and Raju, a young couple who have been married for about two years. Their parents arranged the marriage when Sannamma was 17 and Raju was 24. Sannamma's parents are relatively rich with ten acres of irrigated land, while Raju's are considerably poorer. Raju shares a house with his parents, his brothers, and their wives and children who all live off a five-acre plot of dry land supplemented by intermittent work as wage laborers. Raju received a dowry of 25,000 rupees, which is about half the size of most other dowries paid in the community at the time. A few months into the marriage, he demanded that Sannamma ask her father to send some money so that he could set up a small tea shop. She agreed and her father sent Raju 2,000 rupees, which is what Raju made in four months. About two months later Raju demanded a motorcycle, a considerably larger request well beyond the means of Sannamma's parents. Sannamma passed on the request to her parents who said that they could not afford such a large sum of money. When Raju heard this, he became very angry, hit Sannamma, threw her to the ground, and said that if her parents did not send the money, 'he could not say what might happen to her.' Subsequently, tensions between Sannamma and Raju have increased considerably and she says that she now lives in fear of her life. Her parents send money when they can even though they cannot really afford to keep up with Raju's demands. However, Sannamma refuses to leave her husband and go back to her parents, fearing social isolation.

(Bloch & Rao, 2002, p. 1031)

Despite the disparity between the genders and their general denigration, Indian women have a long history of political activism and have given their voices to political protests, the independence movement, the trade union movement and guerrilla warfare (Mitra, 2004). The commitment of Indian women to political causes was rewarded in 1966 when the first (and to date only) female Prime Minister was elected. Indira Priyadarshini Gandhi (no relation to Mahatma Gandhi) served during 1966–1977 and 1980–1984 when she was assassinated. India also currently has a female president, Pratibha Devisingh Patil, who was elected in 2007. However, despite these successes women in India still remain a much marginalised group (Chowdhury & Patnaik, 2010; Mitra, 2004).

Thus we can see how being born a boy or a girl can have life-threatening implications for Indian children. Girls are less likely to thrive, are less well nourished and are considered by some to be objects which can be bought and sold into marriage. Most importantly girls are less likely to be born in India, with abortion due to sex a common event. On the other hand boys are favoured throughout their lives and are likely to be sexually aggressive towards women. We can see therefore how the development of a child based on sex varies widely in India. While academics in the west often report on the male dominance in the west (e.g. Bem, 1993) the gender disparity in India is much more marked and much more likely to have a significant effect on a child's life course.

Having briefly explored the issue of gender inequality and son preference in India we will now look to Africa and the issues of female genital mutilation (FGM) and the HIV/AIDS crisis which reveal much about attitudes towards the genders.

Africa

Africa is a continent and is made up of over 50 countries and territories; from Algeria at the top of Africa, to South Africa at its tip, from

Somalia in the west and Senegal in the east. The total population estimate is 1.1 billion and it is thought that there are up to 3000 different languages in use across thousands of different tribes and cultural groups. The characteristics of each country are unique, with many subcultures based on tribal heritage, religion and political persuasion within any one country; however due to space constraints we are limited to presenting some general issues which affect the whole continent, rather than looking at the individual countries. We will look at the issue of FGM and the HIV/AIDS crisis. All of these issues are strongly associated with gender and will give an idea that compares growing up in the west and growing up in Africa.

Female genital mutilation

One serious and on-going issue regarding gender in Africa is the phenomenon of FGM and, while it is practised in a number of cultures, it is most prevalent in the African continent. The term refers to any mutilation of female genitalia and the World Health Organisation refers to four different types: partial or complete removal of the clitoris, partial or complete removal of the clitoris and labia minora, narrowing of the vaginal orifice (with or without mutilation of the clitoris) and the final category refers to any other mutilation. FGM serves no medical purpose, causes significant medical and psychological problems and is a culturally sanctioned form of violence against the female body; furthermore the procedure is almost always carried out on infants and children. The mutilation is carried out to diminish or completely remove female sexual enjoyment and, in cases of the narrowing of the vaginal entrance, to ensure that virginity is maintained (at the point of marriage the female requires another procedure to allow intercourse).

Women who have undergone FGM are more likely to suffer from long-term health issues such as higher levels of reproductive tract and urinary tract infections (which can lead to kidney damage), infertility, formation of cysts in the scar tissue and problems during childbirth (Toubia, 1994). It has been found that women who have been victim to FGM are considerably more likely to suffer from poor mental health; in a survey of Senegalese women it was found that 78 per cent had FGM performed without any warning or explanation and over 80 per cent suffered flash-backs regarding the event (Behrendt & Mortiz, 2005).

Despite the serious implications of FGM and its condemnation by the World Health Organisation and other inter-border agencies (such as UNICEF) the practice is still very common, with some African countries experiencing a near 100 per cent mutilation rate for young girls as can be seen in Table 12.1.

COUNTRY	YEAR OF ESTIMATE	PREVALENCE (PERCENTAGE)
Somalia	2006	97.9
Guinea	2005	95.6
Sierra Leone	2006	94
Djibouti	2006	93.1
Egypt	2008	91.1
Sudan (northern)	2000	90
Eritrea	2002	88.7
Mali	2006	85.2
Gambia	2005/2006	78.3
Ethiopia	2005	74.3
Burkina Faso	2006	72.5
Mauritania	2007	72.2
Liberia	2007	58.2
Chad	2004	44.9
Guinea-Bissau	2006	44.5
Côte d'Ivoire	2006	36.4
Nigeria	2008	29.6
Senegal	2005	28.2
Kenya	2008/2009	27.1
Central African Republic	2008	25.7
United Republic of Tanzania	2004	14.6
Benin	2006	12.9
Togo	2006	5.8

Table 12.1 Estimated prevalence of female genital mutilation
Source: World Health Organization (2011).

COUNTRY	YEAR OF ESTIMATE	PREVALENCE (PERCENTAGE)
Ghana	2006	3.8
Niger	2006	2.2
Cameroon	2004	1.4
Uganda	2006	0.8

Table 12.1 (Continued)

These figures translate to 91.5 million women currently living in Africa who have experienced FGM and an estimate of 3 million girls who are experiencing this form of abuse every year (World Health Organization, 2011). While FGM is predominantly practised in Africa, it is becoming increasingly common in more developed societies due to the processes of migration (Momoh et al., 2001). Thus FGM represents a serious issue for women all around the world, but particularly in Africa, and is part of a wider problem regarding how the female body is conceptualised as belonging to men.

The HIV/AIDS crisis

This is a very important topic when considering both gender and child-hood in Africa as the continued spread of the disease is wrapped up in cultural notions of what is to be male and female while children are affected both by the disease itself and through the effects of their parents being ill. Human Immunodeficiency Virus (HIV) is a disease that attacks the immune system and is transmitted through the exchange of bodily fluids (normally during unprotected sex). Acquired Immune Deficiency Syndrome (AIDS) refers to the advanced stages of HIV and occurs when the immune system no longer functions. Once this happens the sufferer contracts serious illnesses, which result in death (such as pneumonia) as the body is no longer able to ward off infection. While there is no cure HIV can be effectively treated with a group of drugs called antiretrovirals; research is currently being conducted into an HIV vaccine, but this remains some years away and the most effective prevention is to practise safe sex and use condoms. HIV/AIDS is a global issue, but the problem is centralised in Africa (particularly sub-Saharan Africa) where the disease has reached epidemic proportions. The following statistics give some idea of just how prevalent the HIV/AIDS crisis is in Africa:

- Nearly 70 per cent of HIV infections and over 75 per cent of deaths from AIDS occur in sub-Saharan Africa (De Cock et al., 2002).
- The leading global cause of disease and death of women (aged 15–49 years) is HIV (UNAIDS, 2010).
- In Africa there are approximately 24 million adults and children who are infected with HIV (WHO, 2010a).
- In 2009 there were approximately two million adults and children who were newly diagnosed with HIV (WHO, 2010a).

Due to differences in gender roles, that is with men dominant partners and women socialised to be subservient and obedient, many women are unable to request that their partners wear condoms; furthermore discussions regarding contraception means that the women would demonstrate knowledge of sexual matters which is in contrast to the cultural demands that women be innocent and unaware of sexual matters (Weiss et al., 2000). Thus the promotion of safe sex is not just a case of access to condoms but involves a complete change in social attitudes.

With regard to the transmission of the disease 1900 children become HIV positive every single day after obtaining the disease from their mother and on average 25–45 per cent of HIV-positive mothers transmit the disease to their children in Africa, compared with just 10–30 per cent in other nations (Dabois & Ekpini, 2002), and 90 per cent of children with HIV live in sub-Saharan Africa (De Cock et al., 2002). There are approximately 600,000 children receiving treatment for their HIV condition, but a further 3 million are in need of treatment (World Health Organisation, 2010b). The problem of HIV among children is now so severe that children in southern Africa now have a shorter life expectancy than their parents (Dabois & Ekpini, 2002). HIV can be passed from mother to child during pregnancy, birth or breastfeeding; some debate still remains with regard to how important breastfeeding is in the transmission of the disease, but it looks like 40 per cent of transmissions could be due to breastfeeding, which is more risky should breast infections (such as mastitis) occur (ibid.). Transmission of the disease can be reduced by use of antiretrovirals, testing of the mother during (or before) pregnancy, counselling and the use of formula feeding; however only about 20 per cent of women tested and counselled begin the pharmaceutical treatment (ibid.). Such programmes however only reach 3 per cent of HIV-infected women in Africa (ibid.); problems with warfare, political unrest, local authorities, funding, access to services by the women and social stigma mean that there is a very large proportion of the population who are currently not receiving treatment.

It is not just the illness itself which is causing problems for Africa, but the after-effects of the illness, such as coping with the vast numbers of children who have lost one or both parents due to the disease. Nine out of ten AIDS orphans live in sub-Saharan Africa (De Cock et al., 2002) and during 1990–2007 approximately 12 million children were orphaned by AIDS across the continent (UNAIDS, 2008). In a 2003 article, Upton describes how the increasing number of orphans due to AIDS is creating a burden of care in Botswana. Botswana is a relatively stable African nation with a democratic government which is active in attempting to curtail the epidemic, yet rates of infection are still high and continue to rise. Upton (2003) draws upon one case study in particular to illustrate just how HIV/AIDS is changing lives:

> Mma Bogadi, who lives in a rural area with limited amenities, has three children of her own but now cares for her late niece's two children as well. She provides them with clothing, food, and school fees and worries about their health given her niece's death from tuberculosis, a clear indication to Mma Bogadi that her niece was HIV positive. The costs of caring for these children are mounting, and rather than the children assisting her in the household, she worries about her resources and abilities to provide for them. Sitting in her three-room cement block home in a rural village in Northern Botswana, Mma Bogadi watches the five young children living in her household as she works on a portable sewing machine, her main source of income.
>
> (p. 316)

This is a story that is repeated across Africa, and the next quote comes from a study conducted in Uganda:

> The 72-year-old woman has two new families to take care of. In the past two years, two of her sons died of AIDS, leaving her with two huts, two shambas and two new sets of mouths to feed. At one side of the village she has three tots between the ages of 1½ and 6. That daughter-in-law left to pursue the possibility of remarriage in Tanzania. Across the ridge are five more kids, the eldest 12 years old. Their mother is believed to be in Mbarara, married again or about to be. The old woman needs blankets, bedding, food and clothing. More than that, she needs to rest from the burden of trying to feed

these children, a task in which she gets no help. And a rest from the psychological burden of knowing she can't provide school fees, the one thing that would enable these kids to avoid ignorance, despondency, eventual juvenile delinquency, the possibilities of becoming criminals or rebels.

(Hunter, 1990, p. 681)

Thus it is not simply a case of reducing incidence of the disease, but dealing with the after-effects and ensuring the care of the children left behind. The burden of care upon relatives is immense and made greater by the possible poor health of the children, high levels of poverty and psychological effects of losing their parent(s).

To summarise the HIV/AIDS epidemic has had a catastrophic effect on Africa and is continuing to do so. Gender plays an important part as cultural stereotypes regarding relationships, sexuality and the subordination of women continue to encourage male promiscuity and a lack of contraception. Childhood is also marred by the epidemic, by the child itself developing HIV/AIDS or by the loss of parents and family through the disease. Again, we can see how the dominance of men and the subordination of women on a cultural level can have great influences upon men and women at an individual level such as dealing with the physical and psychological impacts of FGM and AIDS. To be born a girl in Africa is to be born with a disadvantage unfortunately.

Mosuo, China

In this section we will take a look at a different society in which the females are the dominant gender. In the west and other cultures (India and Africa in particular) we have looked at up to now in this chapter the male gender has been the governing sex, often at the expense of women; yet there are a few societies where this is not the case. One of these societies which has been written about extensively is Mosuo, in the southwest of China (near the border of Tibet). The society is made up of several small villages and hamlets which are scattered around the mountains and totals around 40,000 people. What sets the Mosuo apart from the rest of China, and perhaps the world, is that their society is the closest that currently exists to a matriarchal one.

While family life in our society is based on the presumption that romantic love, in the form of cohabitation or marriage, is the foundation of a strong family unit, the Mosuo, on the other hand, separate their family life and their romantic life. The sexual life of adolescents begins following a ritual as explained below:

> At the age of thirteen, a girl undergoes an initiation 'skirt' ceremony that culminates in receiving a literal sleeping room of her own. In what the Mosuo language terms her 'flower chamber,' she can freely receive (or rebuff) nocturnal visits from any male suitor who comes to call. An analogous 'pants' ceremony marks the cultural passage to maturity for boys who turn thirteen, but they do not receive private sleeping quarters. Instead, mature males become eligible to practice tisese, which the Chinese misleadingly translate as walking marriage ('zuohun'). The Mosuo term, however, literally means that a man 'goes back and forth.' Men live, eat, and work with their maternal families by day, but after nightfall, they can seek entry into the flower chambers of any women they desire.
>
> (Stacey, 2009, pp. 290–291)

There are two forms of 'tisese' among the Mosuo; one which is a casual arrangement and means that the couple meet at night, but do not have an exclusive relationship, and the other involves an exchange of gifts and a more formal relationship and an expectation of exclusivity. With both arrangements however the couple only meet at night with the male returning to his family home in the morning to take up his family duties. As the relationship does not interfere with family life the coupling is based only on sexual or romantic desire. Interestingly there is also no pressure placed on women to conform to sexual ideas regarding chastity, but there is an expectation that the male and female will be equal partners in their liaisons.

As family units are based on the matrilineal line, rather than romantic relationships, there is also a lack of awareness or concern regarding the father of infants (Johnson & Zhang, 1991). A child is raised by its mother's kin, so the child will live with its aunts (its mother's sisters), uncles (its mother's brothers) and grandmother; thus the biological father is of little importance. The child is raised collectively, to the point that the Mosuo word for 'mother' is the same as for 'maternal aunt'; and because of this collective child rearing there is no sense of being without a father. This way of life might be difficult to comprehend as "a more individualistic, modern Western perspective would chafe at the level of conformity to family and social norms that Mosuo kinship demands. It is difficult for mobile, modern Westerners to imagine residing permanently with natal kin" (Stacey, 2009, p. 320). However, it is a way of life that has deep historical roots and is successful in maintaining kinships ties and freeing romantic relationships from the burden of domestic labour; males and females form unions based only on mutual desire and love.

Unfortunately due to cultural changes beyond the Mosuo's control (such as the rise of communism in China) and the increasing infiltration of westernised notions of marriage the Mosuo way of life is becoming endangered. Given the vanishing nature of many traditional forms of Chinese life, 'ethnic museums' have been established where tribal ways are preserved by employing members of ethnic groups to live in a compound and explain their way of life to visiting tourists. Stacey (2009) describes meeting a young man who was employed at such a museum and the peculiar irony that in being employed to preserve his ethnic heritage in fact meant abandoning it and setting up a household as a couple:

> He had lived in his mother Jiama's household, while his 'wife' and their young daughter resided in their separate matrilineal homestead. The employment opportunity at Dongba Valley precipitated a dramatic family change. In order to display 'authentic' Mosuo life for hire, the couple had been compelled to abandon their former traditional walking marriage along with their young daughter, their maternal households and native Mosuo communities and to become an employed cohabiting couple who lived and worked far from their Mosuo homes.
>
> (pp. 312–313)

The idea of 'ethnic museums' is certainly concerning but hints at bigger issues at how to preserve indigenous cultures as they come under increasing pressure to adopt westernised ways of life.

Thus the Mosuo represent a different approach to gender with a concern for matrilineal lines, rather than a patriarchal lineage which in turn has meant an altered attitude to romantic relationships. This is a rare culture though and as such it has attracted enormous attention and the Mosuo are now something of a tourist attraction. It is a successful culture which has been self-sufficient for several centuries, but the encroachment of western notions of family means that it is under threat. In contrast to the earlier examples of India and Africa, to be born a woman in the Mosuo predicts a life of empowerment and equality.

Thinking scientifically → **Coming of age in Samoa**

There is one famous anthropological controversy that highlights the potential research dangers in conducting field work in another culture. Margaret Mead (1901–1979) was an American anthropologist who made a name for herself by conducting ethnographic work in tribal cultures. First published in 1928 'Coming of Age in Samoa' recounted Mead's interpretation of Samoan culture after she spent several months observing local communities. She was particularly interested in the period of adolescence and wanted to see if the Samoan experience of puberty, especially for girls, was similar to the American experience. She reported that Samoan life and adolescence were dramatically different from American society and she placed great emphasis on the idyllic nature of island life (Feinberg, 1988). Mead wrote that the adolescent period for Samoans was not at all similar to that of American youth; there was no anxiety, no search for identity, no confusion and no stress. She also reported that although virginity was highly praised in Samoa there was also a degree of sexual freedom and many of the young women indulged in clandestine affairs before they got married, later concealing their sexual experience; she briefly refers to how young women used chicken's blood to emulate the breaking of the hymen on their wedding night. Mead's book was an immediate success in America and made her one of the most famous anthropologists of all time; most importantly for academics it confirmed the notion that it was nurture that shaped gender, rather than nature. Mead went on to have a very illustrious academic career and published prolifically, with her primary interest remaining the cultural shaping of gender.

In the 1940s Derek Freeman went to Samoa to conduct research, expecting to find similar results to Mead. As his knowledge of Samoan life grew, so did his conviction that Mead had not published an accurate portrayal of the culture. The pair engaged in a long correspondence regarding Mead's work and she came to realise that Samoa was not the sexually liberated paradise she had reported, although she died before the public and academic community was made aware of this. In 1983 Freeman published *Margaret Mead and Samoa: The Making and Unmaking of an Anthropological Myth* in which he detailed a more accurate account of Samoan life and culture. At the time the book was very poorly received by the academic and wider community as, although Mead was deceased, it was seen as a major criticism of a legendary work and a legendary woman. While Mead may have exaggerated some of her claims, it was becoming clear however that she had been fundamentally misled in some of her data collection exercises.

In 1987 Freeman visited Samoa in order to make a documentary regarding Mead's work and met an elderly lady who had taken part in Mead's original study; it was at this point that the mystery unravelled. At the end of her research period Mead was dangerously close to not having sufficient data and so during a long walk on a beach one evening with two young Samoan women she asked them about their sexual experiences. The young women, indulging in the Samoan love of jokes, told Mead of midnight trysts and promiscuity. The elderly woman was rigorously interviewed, had her memory extensively tested and gave a testimony describing what really happened on that fateful night. In 1999 Freeman published *The Fateful Hoaxing of Margaret Mead: A Historical Analysis of Her Samoan Research* which is an overview and analysis of the controversy. Following the deaths of Freeman and Mead (Freeman died in 2001), anthropologists have continued to debate whether one of the most famous researchers was duped and whether one of the most famous ethnographic studies was a fallacy (Marshall, 1993; Shankman, 1996, 2000, 2009).

◉ Chapter summary

In this chapter we have briefly looked at how gender relations and roles are played out in cultures other than western society as it is important that we do not adopt an ethnocentric way of viewing any psychological phenomenon. While there is insufficient space to take anything other than the briefest of views from a handful of cultures, we have examined three cultures in particular which reveal very different ideas of gender. We first looked at India and the impact that son preference has had on gender attitudes, with the important realisation that being female may mean a foetus is not even given a chance at life. We then turned to Africa and the phenomenon of FGM and the HIV/AIDS crisis to explore how cultural notions of gender and sexuality have a significant effect on the health and well-being of women and children. Finally we looked at the Mosuo people from China to explore another way of approaching gender relations; this society, unlike all of the others we have looked at throughout the book, is matrilineal rather than patrilineal. Thus our notion of gender in contemporary UK is a very specific one which is different to the one that exists in other modern societies.

These different cultural environments have a great influence on how the child is raised. Throughout all of the earlier theories regarding gender development the cultural environment has been discussed as being the key to how the child learns to be male or female. Whether following the behaviour of models (as in social learning theory) or through the androcentric lens through which behaviour is viewed (enculturated lens theory) culture and socially approved ways of behaving are crucial to gender development. Thus the wider social environment which dictates how gender is conceptualised cannot be overlooked when considering how gender develops.

◉ Further reading

Dabois, F. & Ekpini, E.R. (2002). HIV-1/AIDS and maternal and child health in Africa. *The Lancet, 359*(9323), 2097–2104.

Ganatra, B., Hirve, S. & Rao, V. N. (2001). Sex-selective abortion: Evidence from a community-based study in Western India. *Asia–Pacific Population Journal, 16*(2), 109–124.

Stacey, J. (2009). Unhitching the horse from the carriage: Love and marriage among the Mosuo. *Utah Law Review, 2,* 287–321.

◉ Key search terms

AIDS
Female Genital Mutilation (or FGM)
Gender and India
HIV
Mosuo
Son preference
Women and India

Notes

1 Introduction

1. Part of Chapter 10 appeared in Franklin, L. (2011). *Parenting and Childhood in a Culture of Fear.* Loughborough University: Unpublished Doctoral Thesis.

Glossary

Adolescence

Adolescence refers to the period of time during which a child progresses through puberty and emerges as an adult.

Androgyny

Androgyny is defined as the demonstration of both male and female characteristics.

Bem Sex Role Inventory

The Bem Sex Role Inventory (1974) is a psychological measure of masculinity, femininity and androgyny. The inventory consists of a list of 60 personality traits (20 stereotypically masculine, 20 feminine and 20 neutral) and the participant is asked to rate (on a seven-point scale) how applicable these terms are to men and women in contemporary society. The results provide the individual with a score for masculinity, femininity and androgyny (the androgyny score refers to how the masculinity and femininity scores interact). There is also a short-form version (Bem, 1981b).

Bullying

Bullying is generally defined as repeated aggressive acts (either verbal or physical) which are committed with the intent to cause harm and occur over a period of time (not just a one-off episode). There must also be a difference in power (either due to social status, age or size) between the bully and victim.

Castration Anxiety

Freud proposed that this was an anxiety that arose during the Oedipus conflict (during the phallic stage). Upon noticing that females do not possess a penis the young boy reasons that they once did, but were castrated. This leads to a castration anxiety on his part as he believes that he too might be castrated. The term can also refer to a metaphorical loss of power; specifically the boy fears that his father will castrate him as he is now a rival for his mother's affections.

Conditioning

This is a type of learning that emerged from the behaviourist school of psychology and refers to the process of learning to associate a stimulus with a behaviour. There are two types of conditioning: classical (where an individual learns to associate one object with another, such as in the case of Pavlov's dogs) and operant (which is based upon behavioural modification through reinforcement, such as reward and punishment).

Ego

The ego begins to develop around the age of two when the infant comes to realise that reality is a limiting factor on the pleasure principle; put simply we cannot have our own way all of the time. The ego develops as a mechanism to bridge the differences between the id's selfish demands and reality. The ego is the hardest working of the three mental structures as it seeks a balance between the selfish id and the altruistic superego.

Electra Conflict

This is the female version of the Oedipus conflict which occurs during the phallic psychosexual stage. During this conflict the girl seeks to create her own identity which is separate to the powerful identity of her mother. She attempts to do this by seeking an ally in her father, but upon realising that he has a penis and she does not (and so develops penis envy) she does not seek him as an ally but as a potential lover. If successful, she reasons, she will be able to own a penis by association and will possess further power if a child is born from their union; thus she consequently re-frames her mother as a rival. This conflict is resolved when the daughter realises that other men can provide her with a penis and a child, thus her desire for her father is repressed and she is able to identify with her mother now that she is no longer a rival.

First-Wave Feminism

First-wave feminism refers to the women's movement in the late nineteenth and early twentieth century which fought for the female right to vote.

Gender Constancy

This is the final stage of gender identity development according to Kohlberg which occurs between 7 and 12 years and occurs when the child realises that their gender is constant and unchangeable.

Gender Dysphoria

This refers to a discomfort about one's biological sex and the associated gendered activities and behaviours.

Gender Identity

According to Kohlberg this is the first stage the child progresses through in terms of their gender development. During this period (age approximately two to three years) the child learns to correctly identify themself as a girl or a boy.

Gender Identity Disorder

A psychiatric diagnosis of Gender Identity Disorder may be given following a persistent and prolonged state of gender dysphoria.

Gender Schema

These are schemas that are particularly associated with a particular sex; for example, we might hold a schema that women are nurses and have long hair, whereas a more appropriate job for a man might be a builder and they are more likely to have shorter hair.

Gender Stability

This occurs between the ages of three and seven according to Kohlberg and is when the child learns that their gender identity is stable (that girls grow up to be women and boys to be men) and is not easily changed, but do not fully appreciate how constant gender is.

Hermaphroditism

Hermaphrodites are individuals who are born with two sets of functioning reproductive organs; one male and one female. Pseudo-hermaphrodites are born with sexual organs of both sexes, but these organs are not capable of reproduction.

Id

According to Freud this is a primeval mental structure which is present from birth. The id is an energetic structure which is concerned with the satisfaction of physical urges, libidos and needs: it is guided by the pleasure principle. At birth this is the only structure that is present and so controls the infants demanding nature. With time the id comes under the control of the ego.

Libido

The libido refers to the energy generated by the id and most commonly refers to sexual energy; libidinal is the adjective form.

Media

The media is defined as any material or source that communicates information to us; thus this includes newspapers, television programmes, newspapers, books and the internet. Due to ever-increasing technology (such as technological developments in mobile phones and increasing mobility of the world wide web) the media is becoming a more prevalent feature of our daily lives.

Modelling

Modelling refers to a learning process where children observe, imitate and adopt the behaviours that are demonstrated by another, particularly those demonstrated by a parent. It has been suggested that there are three main types of modelling: verbal (where the child is given verbal instructions as to how to behave appropriately), live modelling (where a child learns from a real-life person and situation) and symbolic (such as representations of behaviour through the media).

Observational Learning

This is an alternative term for modelling.

Oedipus Conflict

This is the conflict that occurs in young boys during the phallic psychosexual stage (the female version is the Electra conflict). As with the Electra conflict, the Oedipus complex arises as the boy realises the power of his mother in his life and so turns to his father as an ally; in seeking this alliance the boy understands the power of the penis. Once the boy fully understands how powerful his penis makes him he experiences sexual desire for his mother, thus casting his father into the role of rival. However, once his father becomes his competitor he begins to fear that his father will act against him in some way and so develops castration anxiety. Driven by the fear of castration the boy realises that his sexual desire for his mother is both hopeless and dangerous and so represses this attraction. Now his father is no longer a rival, the boy can once again seek him as an ally.

Oestrogen

Oestrogen belongs to the group of hormones called estradiols. It is found in higher levels in women than in men; it is important in the production of secondary characteristics of females during puberty and the female reproductive cycle.

Penis Envy

According to Freud young girls experience penis envy when they are progressing through the Electra conflict. This is said to arise as the young girl realises that she does not possess a penis, but her powerful father does. The young girl associates power with the penis and feels envious that she does not possess this power. Unsurprisingly this concept has been rejected by many modern psychoanalysts as it is based on the notion that the male anatomy is the norm and that the female body is lacking.

Play

Play is most commonly characterised as a behaviour which is not goal-oriented; in essence play is activity which is indulged in only because it is enjoyable. Krasnor and Pepler (1980) identify four features as typical of play behaviours: flexibility, the presence of a positive emotion, a non-literal aspect to the activities and an intrinsic motivation.

Pleasure Principle

This is the motivational force which seeks to satiate libidinal urges.

Progesterone

Progesterone belongs to the same group of hormones as oestrogen. It is found in both males and females, but is particularly important for women where it is significant in the female reproductive cycle.

Psychosexual Stages

These are the stages of development as proposed by Freud. Each stage features libidinal urges focused on a particular area of the body and must be successfully navigated for the development of a healthy adult character, if not particular traits will develop which are associated with each stage (such as neatness and messiness associated with the anal stage). The stages (and approximate ages when they occur) are Oral (birth to 1 year), Anal (1–3 years), Phallic (3–6 years), Latency (6 years to adolescence) and Genital (adolescence to adulthood).

Psychosocial Stages

These were the stages of identity development as proposed by Erikson who emphasised the social, rather than the sexual (as Freud did with his psychosexual stages). The stages (and ages) are: Trust vs. Mistrust (birth to 1 year), Autonomy vs. Shame and Doubt (1–3 years), Initiative vs. Guilt (3–6 years), Industry vs. Inferiority (6–12 years), Identity vs. Role Confusion (12–18 years), Intimacy vs. Isolation (18–30 years), Generativity vs. Stagnation (30 years to late adulthood) and Integrity vs. Despair (late adulthood onwards).

Puberty

Puberty is the period of biological change during which a child undergoes great physical changes and develops an adult body capable of reproduction.

Schema

A schema is a general perception or expectation regarding an object, person, event or behaviour; for example, we have a general idea of what happens when we go shopping or go to the theatre. There are several types of schemas including person schemas, self-schemas, role schemas, and event schemas (also known as scripts).

Second-Wave Feminism

This refers to the feminist movement of the 1960s and 1970s which fought for gender equality.

Sex/Gender Binary

This is a traditional way of thinking which suggests that there are only two sexes: male and female. This has been challenged in recent decades with an increasing awareness of the limitations of only conceptualising of two genders, particularly when one considers the issues concerning hermaphroditism and transsexualism.

Sex Typing

Sex typing refers to the adoption of behaviours, mannerisms and characteristics that are considered gender appropriate. So, for example, a highly sex-typed female might be passive, wear skirts and make-up every day, enjoy providing home-cooked meals for her husband and work in a gendered role, such as a nursery school assistant.

Sexual Dimorphism

This term refers to the visible differences between males and females. It is the sexual dimorphism of external genitalia at birth (or even in the womb via ultrasound) which results in classification as either male or female.

Stereotype

A stereotype is a general idea we hold, based on social norms and schemas, that suggests how an individual belonging to a certain group might behave. We might propose, for example, that a professor is very intelligent, but very unorganised and is likely to have a messy desk or that a black man is likely to be better at sport than a white man.

Superego

The superego is the final mental structure to develop, according to Freud, which occurs at approximately 6 years of age. The superego is the higher moral centre and is concerned with the needs of society, rather than the self. Thus it is the responsibility of the ego to manage these social and altruistic ideals with the demands of both the id and reality.

Temperament

Temperament refers to the physiological reactions, base-lines and rhythms that affect our constitution and character; it is biological and so is innate and present from birth.

Testosterone

Testosterone is a hormone which belongs to the androgen class. It occurs in both men and women, but in much higher levels in men and is particularly important during puberty and the development of secondary sexual characteristics.

Third-Wave Feminism

This is a feminist movement which began in the early 1990s and focuses on the rights of ethnic, impoverished and homosexual women.

Transsexualism

A transsexual is an individual who has undergone or is undergoing surgical gender re-assignment. Following experiences of gender dysphoria or a diagnosis of Gender Identity Disorder an individual may choose to undergo corrective surgery to change their biological sex.

Triadic Reciprocal Causation

Bandura (1986) suggested that there was a triadic reciprocal causation to social learning. This simply refers to the fact that there are three factors which interrelate to affect our motivation to learn; these are behaviour, internal processes and the external environment.

Turner's Syndrome

This is a relatively rare condition when infants are born without a second sex chromosome (i.e. without an X or Y contribution from the sperm). Those individuals with Turner's Syndrome often have external female genitalia, but lack functioning internal female sexual organs.

References

Adams, S., Kuebli, J., Boyle, P. A., & Fivush, R. (1995). Gender differences in parent–child conversations about past emotions: A longitudinal investigation. *Sex Roles, 33*(5/6), 309–323.

Alexander, G. M., Wilcox, T., & Woods, R. (2009). Sex differences in infant's visual interest in toys. *Archives of Sexual Behaviour, 38*(3), 427–433.

American Psychiatric Association (2000). *Diagnostic and statistical manual of mental disorders: DSM-IV-TR*. Washington: American Psychiatric Association.

Anderson, S. (2003). Why dowry payments decline with modernization in Europe, but are rising in India. *Journal of Political Economy, 111*(2), 269–310.

Antaki, C. (2004). Reading minds or dealing with interactional implications? *Theory and Psychology, 14*(5), 667–683.

Archer, J. (1991). The influence of testosterone on human aggression. *British Journal of Psychology, 82*(1), 1–28.

Arnold, F., Kishor, S., & Roy, T. K. (2002). Sex-selective abortions in India. *Population and Development Review, 28*(4), 759–785.

Augoustinos, M. & Walker, I. (1995). *Social cognition: An integrated approach*. London, Thousand Oaks & New Delhi: Sage Publications Ltd.

Bandura, A. (1965). Influence of models' reinforcement contingencies on the acquisition of imitative responses. *Journal of Personality and Social Psychology, 1*(6), 589–595.

Bandura, A. (1969). Social-learning theory of indentificatory processes. In D. A. Goslin (Ed.). *Handbook of socialization theory and research* (pp. 213–262). Chicago, Illinois: Rand McNally and Company.

Bandura, A. (1986). *Social foundations of thought and action: A social cognitive theory*. Englewood Cliffs, New Jersey: Prentice Hall.

Bandura, A. (1997). *Self-efficacy: The exercise of control*. New York: Freeman.

Bandura, A. (2001). Social cognitive theory: An agentic perspective. *Annual Review of Psychology, 52*, 1–26.

Bandura, A. (2002a). Social cognitive theory in cultural context. *Applied Psychology: An International Review, 51*(2), 269–290.

Bandura, A. (2002b). Social cognitive theory of mass communications. In J. Bryant & D. Zilman (Eds). *Media effects: Advances in theory and research*, 2nd Edition (pp. 121–153). Hillsdale, New Jersey: Erlbaum.

Bandura, A. (2003). On the psychosocial impact and mechanisms of spiritual modeling. *The International Journal for the Psychology of Religion, 13*(3), 167–173.

Bandura, A. (2004). Model of causality in social learning theory. In A. Freeman, M. J. Mahoney, P. Devito, & D. Martin (Eds). *Cognition and psychotherapy*, 2nd Edition (pp. 24–44). New York: Springer Publishing Company.

Bandura, A., Ross, D., & Ross, S. A. (1961). Transmission of aggression through imitation of aggressive models. *Journal of Abnormal and Social Psychology, 63*(3), 575–582.

Bandura, A., Ross, D., & Ross, S. A. (1963). Imitation of film-mediated aggressive models. *Journal of Abnormal and Social Psychology, 66*(1), 3–11.

Barberá, E. (2003). Gender schemas: Configuration and activation processes. *Canadian Journal of Behavioural Science, 35*(3), 176–184.

Baron-Cohen, S., Knickmeyer, R. C., & Belmonte, M. K. (2005). Sex differences in the brain: Implications for explaining autism. *Science, 310*, 919–823.

Bartlett, N. H. & Vasey, P. L. (2006). A retrospective study of childhood gender-atypical behaviour in Samoan fa'afafine. *Archives of Sexual Behavior, 35*(6), 659–666.

Behrendt, A. & Moritz, S. (2005). Posttraumatic stress disorder and memory problems after female genital mutilation. *American Journal of Psychiatry, 162*(5), 1000–1002.

Bem, S. L. (1974). The measurement of psychological androgyny. *Journal of Consulting and Clinical Psychology, 42*(2), 155–162.

Bem, S. L. (1981a). Gender schema theory: A cognitive account of sex typing. *Psychological Review, 88*(4), 354–364.

Bem, S. L. (1981b). *Bem sex role inventory: Professional manual.* Palo Alto, California: Consulting Psychologists Press.

Bem, S. L. (1983). Gender schema theory and its implications for child development: Raising gender aschematic children in a gender-schematic society. *Signs, 8*(4), 598–616.

Bem, S. L. (1989). Genital knowledge and gender constancy in preschool children. *Child Development, 60,* 642–649.

Bem, S. L. (1993). *The lenses of gender: Transforming the debate on sexual inequality.* New Haven and London: Yale University Press.

Bem, S. L. (1994). Defending the lenses of gender. *Psychological Inquiry, 5*(1), 97–101.

Bem, S. L. (2001). *An unconventional family.* New Haven and London: Yale University Press.

Blackless, M., Charuvastra, A., Derryck, A., Fausto-Sterling, A., Lauzannr, K., & Lee, E. (2000). How sexually dimorphic are we? Review and synthesis. *American Journal of Human Biology, 12*(2), 151–166.

Blakemore, J. E. O. (1990). Children's nurturant interactions with their infant siblings: An exploration of gender differences and maternal socialisation. *Sex Roles, 22*(1/2), 43–57.

Bloch, F. & Rao, V. (2002). Terror as a bargaining instrument: A case study of dowry violence in rural India. *The American Economic Review, 92*(4), 1029–1043.

Block, J. H. (1976). Issues, problems, and pitfalls in assessing sex differences: A critical review of 'The Psychology of Sex Differences'. *Journal of Developmental Psychology, 22*(4), 283–308.

Boldizar, J. P. (1991). Assessing sex typing and androgyny in children: The children's sex role inventory. *Developmental Psychology, 27*(3), 505–515.

Book, A. S., Starzyk, K. B., & Quinsey, V. L. (2001). The relationship between testosterone and aggression: A meta-analysis. *Aggression and Violent Behaviour, 6*(6), 579–599.

Borenstein, J. E., Dean, B. B., Endicott, J., Wong, J., Brown, C., Dickerson, V., & Yonkers, K. A. (2003). Health and economic impact of the premenstrual syndrome. *Journal of Reproductive Medicine, 48*(7), 515–524.

Borooah, V. K. (2004). Gender bias among children in India in their diet and immunization against disease. *Social Science & Medicine, 58*(9), 1719–1731.

Borzekowski, D. L. G., Robinson, T. N., & Killen, J. D. (2000). Does the camera add 10 pounds? Media use, perceived importance of appearance, and weight concerns among teenage girls. *Journal of Adolescent Health, 26*(1), 36–41.

Brady, G., Brown, G., Letherby, G., Bayley, J., & Wallace, L. M. (2008). Young women's experience of termination and miscarriage: A qualitative study. *Human Fertility, 11*(3), 186–190.

Bremner, J. D., Staib, L. H., Kaloupek, D., Southwick, S. M., Soufer, R., & Charney, D. S. (1999). Neural correlates of exposure to traumatic pictures and sound in Vietnam combat veterans with and without posttraumatic stress disorder: A positron emission tomography study. *Biological Psychiatry, 45*(7), 806–816.

Brookes, H., Slater, A., Quinn, P. C., Lewkowicz, D. J., Hayes, R., & Brown, E. (2001). Three-month-old infants learn arbitrary auditory-visual pairings between voices and faces. *Infant and Child Development, 10*(1–2), 75–82.

Brownell, K. D. & Napolitano, M. A. (1995). Distorting reality for children: Body size proportions of Barbie and Ken Dolls. *International Journal of Eating Disorders, 18*(3), 295–298.

Buchmann, C., DiPrete, T. A., & McDaniel, A. (2008). Gender inequalities in education. *Annual Review of Sociology, 34*, 319–337.

Bunting, L. & McAuley, C. (2004). Research review: teenage pregnancy and parenthood: The role of fathers. *Child and Family Social Work, 9*(3), 295–303.

Burr, V. (1998). *Gender and social psychology.* London: Routledge.

Burr, V. (2003). *Social constructionism*, 2nd Edition. London and New York: Routledge.

Buss, D. M. (1994). *The evolution of desire.* New York: Basic Books.

Buss, D. M. (2000). *The dangerous passion: Why jealousy is as necessary as love and sex.* New York: The Free Press.

Buss, D. M. (2012). *Evolutionary psychology: The new science of the mind*, 4th Edition. Boston, Massachusetts: Allyn & Bacon.

Bussey, K. & Bandura, A. (1984). Influence of gender constancy and social power on sex-linked modeling. *Journal of Personality and Social Psychology, 47*(6), 1291–1302.

Bussey, K. & Bandura, A. (1992). Self-regulatory mechanisms governing gender development. *Child Development, 63*(5), 1236–1250.

Bussey, K. & Bandura, A. (1999). Social-cognitive theory of gender development and differentiation. *Psychological Review, 10*(4), 676–713.

Butcher, J. N., Mineka, S., & Hooley, J. M. (2008). *Abnormal psychology: Core concepts*, 2nd Edition. Boston, Massachusetts: Pearson Education.

Caldera, Y. M., Huston, A. C., & O'Brien, M. (1989). Social interactions and play patterns of parents and toddlers with feminine, masculine and neutral toys. *Child Development, 60*(1), 70–76.

Campbell, A., Shirley, L., & Candy, J. (2004). A longitudinal study of gender-related cognition and behaviour. *Developmental Science, 7*(1), 1–9.

Campbell, A., Shirley, L., Heywood, C., & Crook, C. (2000). Infants' visual preferences for sex-congruent babies, children, toys and activities: A longitudinal study. *British Journal of Developmental Psychology, 18*(4), 479–498.

Carli, L. L. (1990). Gender, language and influence. *Journal of Personality and Social Psychology, 59*(5), 941–951.

Carlson, S. M. & Taylor, M. (2005). Imaginary companions and impersonated characters: Sex differences in children's fantasy play. *Merrill-Palmer Quarterly, 51*(1), 93–118.

Carver, K., Joyner, K., & Udry, J. R. (2003). National estimates of adolescent romantic relationships. In P. Florsheim (Ed.). *Adolescent romantic relations and sexual behaviour: Theory, research and practical implications* (pp. 23–56). Mahwah, New Jersey: Lawrence Erlbaum.

Cherney, I. D. & London, K. (2006). Gender-linked differences in the toys, television shows, computer games, and outdoor activities of 5- to 13-year-old children. *Sex Roles, 54*(9/10), 717–726.

Chodorow, N. J. (1995). Gender as a personal and social construct. *Signs, 20*(3), 516–544.

Chowdhury, A. & Patnaik, M. M. (2010). Empowering boys and men to achieve gender inequality in India. *Journal of Developing Societies, 26*(4), 455–471.

Cohen-Kettenis, P. T., Owen, A., Kaijser, V. G.,Bradley, S. J., & Zucker, K. J. (2003). Demographic characteristics, social competence, and behavior problems in children with gender identity disorder: A cross-national, cross-clinic comparative analysis. *Journal of Abnormal Child Psychology, 31*(1), 41–53.

Colapinto, J. (1997). The true story of John Joan. *Rolling Stone*, December, 54–72, 92, 94–97.

Collins, W. A. (2003). More than myth: The developmental significance of romantic relationships during adolescence. *Journal of Research on Adolescence, 13*(1), 1–24.

Connolly, J. & Johnson, A. (1996). Adolescents' romantic relationships and the structure and quality of their close interpersonal ties. *Personal Relationships, 3*(2), 185–195.

Cooper, C. A., McCord, D. M., & Socha, A. (2011). Evaluating the college sophomore problem: The case of personality and politics. *The Journal of Psychology, 145*(1), 23–37.

Cosgrove, K. P., Mazure, C. M., & Staley, J. K. (2007). Evolving knowledge of sex differences in brain structure, function and chemistry. *Biological Psychiatry, 62*(8), 847–855.

Cromby, J. (2004). Between constructionism and neuroscience: The societal co-constitution of embodied subjectivity. *Theory and Psychology, 14*(6), 797–821.

Cromby, J. (2007). Toward a psychology of feeling. *International Journal of Critical Psychology, 21*, 94–118.

Crouter, A. C., Manke, B. A., & McHale, S. M. (1995). The family context of gender intensification in early adolescence. *Child Development, 66*(2), 317–329.

Crowther, K. M. (2010). *Adam and Eve in the protestant reformation.* New York: Cambridge University Press.

Dabois, F. & Ekpini, E. R. (2002). HIV-1/AIDS and maternal and child health in Africa. *The Lancet, 359*(9323), 2097–2104.

Damon, W. (1977). *The social world of the child.* San Francisco, California: Josey Bass.

De Cock, K. M., Mbori-Ngacha, D., & Marum, E. (2002). Shadow on the continent: Public health and HIV/AIDS in Africa in the 21st century. *The Lancet, 360*(9326), 67–72.

De Gaston, J. & Weed, S. (1996). Understanding gender differences in adolescent sexuality. *Adolescence, 31*(121), 217–231.

Deaux, K. (1994). Review: Whose debate is it anyway? *Psychological Inquiry, 5*(1), 80–96.

Dee, T. S. (2007). Teachers and the gender gaps in student achievement. *Journal of Human Resources, 42*(3), 528–554.

Delk, J. L., Maden, R. B., Livingston, M., & Ryan, T. T. (1986). Adult perceptions of the infant as a function of gender labelling and observer gender. *Sex Roles, 15*(9/10), 527–534.

Department for Education (2010). *GCSE and equivalent results in England 2009/2010 (SFR 30/2010)*. London, England: Department for Education.

Department for Education (2010a). *Key Stage 1 Attainment by pupil characteristics, in England 2009/2010 (SFR 33/2010)*. London: Department for Education.

Department for Education (2010b). *Key Stage 2 Attainment by pupil characteristics, in England 2009/2010 (SFR 35/2010)*. London: Department for Education.

Department for Education (2011). *GCE/Applied GCSE A/AS and equivalent examination results in England, 2009/2010 (Revised) (SFR 02/2011)*. London, England: Department for Education.

DeWalt, D. A., Berkman, N. D., Sheridan, S., Lohr, K. N., & Pignone, M. P. (2004). Literacy and health outcomes: A systematic review of the literature. *Journal of General Internal Medicine, 19*(12), 1228–1239.

Diamond, M. & Sigmundson, K. (1997). Sex reassignment at birth: Long-term review and clinical implications. *Archives of Pediatrics and Adolescent Medicine, 151*(3), 298–304.

Dietz, T. L. (1998). An examination of violence and gender role portrayals in video games: Implications for gender socialization and aggressive behaviour. *Sex Roles, 38*(5/6), 425–442.

DiPietro, J. A. (1981). Rough and tumble play: A function of gender. *Developmental Psychology, 17*(1), 50–58.

Douvan, E. & Adelson, J. (1966). *The adolescent experience.* New York: Wiley.

Dreger, A. D. (1998). *Hermaphrodites and the medical invention of sex.* Cambridge, Massachusetts: Harvard University Press.

Drummond, K. D., Bradley, S. J., Peterson-Badali, M., & Zucker, K. J. (2008). A follow-up study of girls with gender identity disorder. *Developmental Psychology, 44*(1), 34–45.

Duffy, J., Warren, K., & Walsh, M. (2001). Classroom interactions: Gender of teacher, gender of student, and classroom subject. *Sex Roles, 45*(9/10), 579–593.

Dunn, J., Bretherton, I., & Munn, P. (1987). Conversations about feeling states between mothers and their young. *Developmental Psychology, 23*(1), 132–139.

Dunn, J., Slomkowski, C., & Beardsall, L. (1994). Sibling relationships from the preschool period through middle childhood and early adolescence. *Developmental Psychology, 30*(3), 315–324.

DuRant, R. H., Krowchuk, D. P., & Sinal, S. H. (1998). Victimization, use of violence, and drug use at school among male adolescents who engage in same-sex sexual behaviour. *The Journal of Pediatrics, 133*(1), 113–118.

Eaton, W. O. & Von Bargen, D. (1981). Asynchronous development of gender understanding in preschool children. *Child Development, 52*, 1020–1027.

Eccles, J. S. & Blumenfeld, P. (1985) Classroom experiences and student gender: Are there differences and do they matter? In L. C. Wilkinson & C. B. Marrett (Eds). *Gender influences in classroom interaction* (pp. 79–114). Orlando, Florida: Academic Press Inc.

Eckert, P. & McConnell-Ginet, S. (2003). *Language and gender.* Cambridge: Cambridge University Press.

Else-Quest, N. M., Hyde, J. S., & Linn, M. C. (2010). Cross-national patterns of gender differences in mathematics: A meta-analysis. *Psychological Bulletin, 136*(1), 103–127.

Else-Quest, N. M., Hyde, J. S., Goldsmith, H. H., & Van Hulle, C. A. (2006). Gender differences in temperament: A meta-analysis. *Psychological Bulletin, 132*(1), 33–72.

Elwood, J. (1999). Equity issues in performance assessment: The contribution of teacher-assessed coursework to gender-related differences in examination performance. *Educational Research and Evaluation, 5*(4), 321–344.

Ember, C. R. (1973). Feminine task assignment and the social behaviour of boys. *Ethos, 1*(4), 424–439.

Emmerich, W., Goldman, K., Kirsh, B., & Sharabany, R (1977). Evidence for a transitional phase in the development of gender constancy. *Child Development, 48*(3), 930–936.

Erikson, E. (1964). Inner and outer space: Reflections on womanhood. *Daedalus, 93*(2), 582–606.

Etaugh, C., Grinnell, K., & Etaugh, A. (1989). Development of gender labelling: Effect of age of pictured children. *Sex Roles, 21*(11/12), 769–773.

Fagot, B. I. (1978). The influences of sex of child in parental reaction to toddler children. *Child Development, 49*(2), 459–465.

Fausto-Sterling, A. (1993). The five sexes: Why male and female are not enough. *The Sciences*, March/April, 20–25.

Fausto-Sterling, A. (2000a). The five sexes: Revisited. *The Sciences*, July/August, 18–23.

Fausto-Sterling, A. (2000b). The sex/gender perplex. *Studies in History and Philosophy of Biological and Biomedical Sciences, 31*(4), 637–646.

Fein, G. G. (1981). Pretend play in childhood: An integrative review. *Child Development, 52*(4), 1095–1118.

Feinberg, R. (1988). Margaret Mead and Samoa: Coming of age in fact and fiction. *American Anthropologist, 90*(3), 656–663.

Fering, C. (1999). Other-sex friendship networks and the development of romantic relationships in adolescence. *Journal of Youth and Adolescence, 28*(4), 495–512.

Fitzpatrick, M. J. & McPherson, B. J. (2010). Coloring within the lines: Gender stereotypes in contemporary coloring books. *Sex Roles, 62*(1/2), 127–137.

Fivush, R. (1989). Exploring sex differences in the emotional content of mother-child conversations about the past. *Sex Roles, 20*(11/12), 675–691.

Fivush, R., Brotman, M. A., Buckner, J. P., & Goodman, S. H. (2000). Gender differences in parent-child narratives. *Sex Roles, 42*(3/4), 233–253.

Forero, R., McLellan, L., Rissel, C., & Bauman, A. (1999). Bullying behaviour and psychosocial health among school students in New South Wales, Australia: Cross sectional survey. *British Medical Journal, 319*(7206), 344–348.

Freeman, D. (1999). *The fateful hoaxing of Margaret Mead: A historical analysis of her Samoan research.* Boulder, Colorado: Westview Press.

French, J. & French, P. (1984). Gender imbalances in the primary classroom: An interactional account. *Educational Research, 26*(2), 127–136.

Freud, S. (1925/2002). Some psychological consequences of the anatomical distinction between the sexes. In R. Adams & D. Savran (Eds). *The masculinity studies reader* (pp. 14–20). Malden, Massachusetts and Oxford, England: Blackwell Publishers Ltd.

Frisch, H. L. (1977). Sex stereotypes in adult-infant play. *Child Development, 48*(4), 1671–1675.

Furman, W. & Buhrmester, D. (1985). Children's perceptions of the qualities of sibling relationships. *Child Development, 56*(2), 448–461.

Furnham, A. & Bitar, N. (1993). The stereotypes portrayal of men and women in British television advertisements. *Sex Roles, 29*(3/4), 297–310.

Ganatra, B., Hirve, S., & Rao, V. N. (2001). Sex-selective abortion: Evidence from a community-based study in Western India. *Asia-Pacific Population Journal, 16*(2), 109–124.

Garner, D. M., Garfinkel, P. E., Schwartz, D., & Thompson, M. (1980). Cultural expectations of thinness in women. *Psychological Reports, 47*(2), 483–491.

Gartstein, M. A. & Rothbart, M. K. (2003). Studying infant temperament via the Revised Infant Behavior Questionnaire. *Infant Behavior and Development, 26*(1), 64–86.

Gartstein, M. A., Slobodskaya, H. R., Żylicz, P. O., Gosztyla, D., & Nakagawa, A. (2010). A cross-cultural evaluation of temperament: Japan, USA, Poland and Russia. *International Journal of Psychology and Psychological Therapy, 10*(1), 55–75.

Gentry, M., Gable, R. K., & Rizza, M. G. (2002). Students' perceptions of classroom activities: Are there grade-level and gender differences? *Journal of Educational Psychology, 94*(3), 539–544.

Gergen, K. (1973). Social psychology as history. *Journal of Personality and Social Psychology, 26*(2), 309–320.

Gergen, K. J. (1985). The social constructionist movement in psychology. *American Psychologist, 40*(3), 266–275.

Gilligan, C. (1993). *In a different voice: Psychological theory and women's development.* Cambridge, Massachusetts and London, England: Harvard University Press.

Gillis, S., Howie, G., & Munford, R. (2004). *Third wave feminism: A critical exploration.* Basingstoke, Hampshire: Palgrave Macmillan.

Ginsburg, G. S. & Silverman, W. K. (2000). Gender role orientation and fearfulness in children with anxiety disorders. *Journal of Anxiety Disorders, 14*(1), 57–67.

Glover, D., Gough, G., Johnson, M., & Cartwright, N. (2000). Bullying in 25 secondary schools: Incidence, impact and intervention. *Educational Research, 42*(2), 141–156.

Goffman, E. (1979). *Gender advertisements.* London: Macmillan.

Goldin, C. & Katz, L. F. (2000). Career and marriage in the age of the pill. *The American Economic Review, 90*(2), 461–465.

Golombok, S. & Tasker, F. (1996). Do parents influence the sexual orientation of their children? Findings from a longitudinal study of lesbian families. *Developmental Psychology, 32*(1), 3–11.

Golombok, S., Spencer, A., & Rutter, M. (1983). Children in lesbian and single-parent households: Psychosexual and psychiatric appraisal. *Journal of Child Psychology and Psychiatry*, *24*(4), 551–572.

Green, R. (1987). *The 'sissy boy syndrome' and the development of homosexuality*. New Haven and London: Yale University Press.

Green, R. (2000). Family cooccurence of 'Gender Dysphoria': Ten sibling or parent-child pairs. *Archives of Sexual Behavior, 29*(5), 499–507.

Gullone, E. (2000). The development of normal fear: A century of research. *Clinical Psychology Review, 20*(4), 429–451.

Guttenplan, S. (Ed.) (1994). *A companion to the philosophy of mind.* Oxford, England and Malden, Massachusetts: Blackwell Publishers Inc.

Hall, C. S. (1954). *A primer of Freudian psychology.* Cleveland, Ohio: World Publishing Co.

Hank, K. (2007). Parental gender preferences and reproductive behaviour: A review of the recent literature. *Journal of Biosocial Science, 39*(5), 759–767.

Harré, R. (2002). *Cognitive science: A philosophical introduction.* London: Sage Publications.

Harris, A. C. (1994). Ethnicity as a determinant of sex role identity: A replication study of item selection of the Bem Sex Role Inventory. *Sex Roles, 31*(3/4), 241–273.

Harrison, T. W. (2003). Adolescent homosexuality and concerns regarding disclosure. *Journal of School Health, 73*(3), 107–112.

Harter, S. & Whitesell, N. R. (1989). Developmental changes in children's understanding of single, multiple, and blended emotion concepts. In C. Saarni & P. L. Harris (Eds). *Children's understanding of emotion* (pp. 81–116). Cambridge, New York, and Melbourne: Cambridge University Press.

Hartman, M. (1976). A descriptive study of the language of men and women born in Maine around 1900 as it reflects the Lakoff hypothesis in 'Language and women's place'. In B. L. Dubois & I. Crouch (Eds). *The sociology of the languages of American women* (pp. 81–90). San Antonio, Texas: Trinity University Press.

Hausman, B. (2000). Do boys have to be boys? Gender, narrativity and the John/Joan case. *Feminist Formations, 12*(3), 114–138.

Hayes, S. & Tantless-Dunn, S. (2010). Am I too fat to be a princess? Examining the effects of popular children's media on young girls' body image. *British Journal of Developmental Psychology, 28*(2), 413–426.

Hird, M. (2000). Gender's nature: Intersexuality, transsexualism and the 'sex/gender' binary. *Feminist Theory, 1*(3), 347–364.

Hoffman, L. W. (1977). Changes in family roles, socialization, and sex differences. *American Psychologist, 32*(8), 644–657.

Hogg, M. A. & Vaughan, G. M. (2005). *Social psychology*, 4th Edition. Essex, England: Pearson Education Ltd.

Holt, C. L. & Ellis, J. B. (1998). Assessing the current validity of the Bem Sex-Role Inventory. *Sex Roles, 39*(11/12), 929–941.

Horney, K. (1923/1967). *Feminine psychology* (Ed. H. Kelman). New York: W. W. Norton.

Horney, K. (1932). The dread of woman. *International Journal of Psychoanalysis, 13*, 348–360.

Horton, K. I., Olds, T. S., Olive, S., & Dank, S. (1996). Ken and Barbie at life size. *Sex Roles, 34*(3/4), 287–294.

Hunter, S. S. (1990). Orphans as a window on the AIDS epidemic in Sub-Saharan Africa: Initial results and implications of a study in Uganda. *Social Science & Medicine, 31*(6), 681–690.

Hyde, J. S., Lindberg, S. M., Linn, M. C., Ellis, A. B., & Williams, C. C. (2008). Gender similarities characterize maths performance. *Science, 321*, 494–495.

Imamura, M., Tucker, J., Hannaford, P., da Silva, M. O., Astin, M., Wyness, L., Bloemenkamp, K. W. M., Jahn, A., Karro, H., Olsen, J., & Temmerman, M. (2007). Factors associated with teenage pregnancy in the European Union countries: A systematic review. *European Journal of Public Health, 17*(6), 630–636.

Jha, P., Kumar, R., Vasa, P., Dhingra, N., Thiruchelvam, D., & Moineddin, R. (2006). Low male-to-female sex ratio of children born in India: National survey of 1.1 million households. *The Lancet, 367*(9506), 211–218.

Johnson, N. E. & Zhang, K.-T. (1991). Matriarchy, polyandry, and fertility amongst the Mosuos in China. *Journal of Biosocial Science, 23*(4), 499–505.

Jones, A. & Glenn, S. M. (1991). Gender differences in pretend play in a primary school group. *Early Child Development and Care, 77*(1), 127–135.

Jungworth, H. (1991). Interaction and gender – Findings of a microethnographical approach to classroom discourse. *Educational Studies in Mathematics, 22*(3), 263–284.

Juvonen, J., Graham, S., & Schuster, M. A. (2003). Bullying among young adolescents: The strong, the weak, and the troubled. *Pediatrics, 112*(6), 1231–1237.

Kahn, M. (2002). *Basic Freud: Psychoanalytic thought for the twenty first century.* New York: Basic Books.

Kalil, A., Ziol-Guest, K. M., & Coley, R. L. (2005). Perceptions of father involvement patterns in teenage-mother families: Predictors and links to mothers' psychological adjustment. *Family Relations, 54*(2), 197–211.

Karraker, K. H., Vogel, D. A., & Lake, M. A. (1995). Parents' gender-stereotyped perceptions of newborns: *The eye of the beholder revisited. Sex Roles, 33*(9/10), 687–701.

Katsurada, E. & Sugihara, Y. (1999). A preliminary validation of the Bem Sex Role Inventory. *Journal of Cross-Cultural Psychology, 30*(5), 641–645.

Kerig, P. K., Cowan, P. A., & Cowan, C. P. (1993). Marital quality and gender differences in parent-child interaction. *Developmental Psychology, 29*(6), 931–939.

Kessler, S. (1998). *Lessons from the intersexed.* New Brunswick: Rutgers University Press.

Kim, Y. S. Koh, Y-J., & Leventhal, B. L. (2004). Prevalence of school bullying in Korean middle school students. *Archives of Pediatrics & Adolescent Medicine, 158*(8), 737–741.

Kirkman, M., Rosenthal, D., and Smith, A. M. A. (1998). Adolescent sex and the romantic narrative: Why some young heterosexuals use condoms to prevent pregnancy but not disease. *Psychology, Health & Medicine, 3*(4), 355–370.

Klein, M. (1957). *Envy and gratitude.* London: Tavistock

Knight, J. L. & Giuliano, T. A. (2001). He's a Laker; She's a 'looker': The consequences of gender-stereotyped portrayals of male and female athletes by the print media. *Sex Roles, 45*(3/4), 217–229.

Kohlberg, L. (1966). A cognitive-developmental analysis of children's sex-role concepts and attitudes. In E. E. Maccoby (Ed.). *The development of sex differences* (pp. 82–172). Stanford, California: Stanford University Press.

Kourany, R. F. C. (1987). Suicide among homosexual adolescents. *Journal of Homosexuality, 13*(4), 111–117.

Krasnor, L. R. & Pepler, D. J. (1980). The study of children's play: Some suggested future directions. *New Directions for Child and Adolescent Development, 1980*9(9), 85–95.

Kuebli, J. & Fivush, R. (1992). Gender differences in parent-child conversations about past emotions. *Sex Roles, 27*(11/12), 683–698.

La Freniere, P., Strayer, F. F., & Gauthier, R. (1984). The emergence of same-sex affiliative preferences among pre-school peers: A developmental/ethological perspective. *Child Development, 55*(5), 1958–1965.

Lamb, M. E., Frodi, M., Hwang, C. P, & Frodi, A. M. (1983). Effects of paternal involvement on infant preferences for mothers and fathers. *Child Development, 54*(2), 450–458.

Lambert, T. W., Goldacre, M. J., & Parkhouse, J. (1998). Doctors who qualified in the UK between 1974 and 1993: Age, gender, nationality, marital status and family formation. *Medical Education, 32*(5), 533–537.

Leaper, C. (2000). Gender, affiliation, assertion, and the interactive context of parent-child play. *Developmental Psychology, 36*(3), 381–393.

Leaper, C. (2000). The social construction and socialization of gender during development. In P. H. Miller and E. K. Scholnick (Eds). *Towards a feminist developmental psychology* (pp. 127–152). New York and London: Routledge.

Leaper, C., Anderson, K. J., & Sanders, P. (1998). Moderators of gender effects on parents' talk to their children: A meta-analysis. *Developmental Psychology, 34*(1), 3–27.

Lebson, M. (2002). Suicide among homosexual youth. *Journal of Homosexuality, 42*(4), 107–117.

Lindberg, S. M., Hyde, J. S., Petersen, J. L., & Linn, M. C. (2010). New trends in gender and mathematics performance: A meta-analysis. *Psychological Bulletin, 136*(6), 1123–1135.

Lorber, J. (1994). *Paradoxes of gender.* New Haven and London: Yale University Press.

Maccoby, E. E. & Jacklin, C. N. (1974). *The psychology of sex differences.* Stanford, California: Stanford University Press.

MacDonald, K. & Parke, R. D. (1986). Parent-child physical play: The effects of sex and age of children and parents. *Sex Roles, 15*(7/8), 367–378.

Marleau, J. D. & Saucier, J.-F. (2002). Preference for a first-born boy in western societies. *Journal of Biosocial Science, 34*(1), 13–27.

Marsh, J. (2000). 'But I want to fly too!': Girls and superhero play in the infant classroom. *Gender and Education, 12*(2), 209–220.

Marshall, M. (1993). The wizard from Oz meets the wicked witch of the East: Freeman, Mead, and ethnographic authority. *American Ethnologist, 20*(3), 604–617.

Martin, C. L. (1989). Children's use of gender-related information in making social judgements. *Developmental Psychology, 25*(1), 80–88.

Martin, C. L. (1993). New directions for investigating children's gender knowledge. *Developmental Review, 13*(2), 184–204

Martin, C. L. & Halverson, C. F. (1981). A schematic processing model of sex typing and stereotyping in young children. *Child Development, 52*(4), 1119–1134.

Martin, C. L. & Ruble, D. (2004). Children's search for gender clues: Cognitive perspectives on gender development. *Current Directions in Psychological Science, 13*(2), 67–70.

Martin, C. L., Ruble, D. N., & Szkrybalo, J. (2002). Cognitive theories of early gender development. *Psychological Bulletin, 128*(6), 930–933.

Martin, E. (1991). The egg and the sperm: How science has constructed a romance based on stereotypical male-female roles. *Signs, 16*(3), 485–501.

Martínez-González, M. A., Gual, P., Lahortiga, F., Alonso, Y., de Irala-Estévez, J., & Cervera, S. (2003). Parental factors, mass media influences, and the onset of eating disorders in a prospective population-based cohort. *Pediatrics, 111*(2), 315–320.

Maziade, M., Côté, R., Boudreault, M., Thivierge, J., & Caperaa, P. (1984). The New York longitudinal model of temperament: Gender differences and demographic correlates in a French-speaking population. *Journal of the American Academy of Child Psychiatry, 23*(5), 582–587.

McCrae, R. R., Costa Jr., P. T., Ostendorf, F., Angleitner, A., Hřebíčková, M., Avia, M. D., Sanz, J., Sánchez-Bernardos, M. L., Kusdil, M. E., Woodfield, R., Saunders, P. R., & Smith, P. B. (2000). Nature over nurture: Temperament, personality, and life span development. *Journal of Personality and Social Psychology, 78*(1), 173–186.

McElvaine, R. S. (2000). *Eve's seed: Biology, the sexes and the course of history.* New York: McGraw Hill.

McHale, S. M. & Crouter, A. C. (2003). How do children exert an impact on family life? In A. C. Crouter & A. Booth (Eds). *Children's influence on family dynamics: The neglected side of family relationships* (pp. 207–220). Mahwah, New Jersey: Lawrence Erlbaum Associates.

McNelles, L. R. & Connolly, J. A. (1999). Intimacy between adolescent friends: Age and gender differences in intimate affect and intimate behaviors. *Journal of Research on Adolescence, 9*(2), 143–159.

Miller, P. H. (2011). *Theories of Developmental Psychology*, 5th Edition. New York: Worth Publishers.

Mischel, W. (1966). A social learning view of sex differences in behaviour. In E. Maccoby (Ed.). *The development of sex differences* (pp. 57–81). Stanford, California: Stanford University Press.

Mitchell, S. A. & Black, M. J. (1995). *Beyond Freud: A history of modern psychoanalytic thought*. New York: Basic Books.

Mitra, A. (2004). Voices of the marginalized on the internet: Examples from a website for women of South Asia. *Journal of Communication, 54*(3), 492–510.

Moller, L. C. & Serbin, L. A. (1996). Antecedents of toddler gender segregation: Cognitive consonance, gender-typed toy preferences and behavioural compatibility. *Sex Roles, 35*(7/8), 445–460.

Momoh, C., Ladhani, S., Lochrie, D. P., & Rymer, J. (2001). Female genital mutilation: Analysis of the first twelve months of a southeast London specialist clinic. *BJOG: An International Journal of Obstetrics & Gynaecology, 108*(2), 186–191.

Money, J. & Ehrhardt, A. (1972). *Man and woman, boy and girl*. Baltimore, MD: John Hopkins Press.

Montirosso, R., Cossi, P., Putnam, S. P., Gartstein, M. A., & Borgatti, R. (2011). Studying cross-cultural differences in temperament in the first year of life: United States and Italy. *International Journal of Behavioural Development, 35*(1), 27–37.

Münte, T. F., Altenmüller, E., & Jäncke, L. (2002). The musician's brain as a model of neuroplasticity. *Nature Reviews Neuroscience, 3*(6), 473–478.

Mutharayappa, R., Choe, M. K., Arnold, F., & Roy, T. K. (1997). *Son preference and its effect on fertility in India*. National Family Health Survey Subject Report No. 3. Mumbai: IIPS.

Myers, C. D., Tsao, J. C. I., Glover, D. A., Kim, S. C., Turk, N., & Zeltzer, L. K. (2006). Sex, gender and age: Contributions to laboratory pain responding in children and adolescents. *The Journal of Pain, 7*(8), 556–564.

Neemann, J., Hubbard, J., & Masten, A. S. (1995). The changing importance of romantic relationship involvement to competence from late childhood to late adolescence. *Development and Psychopathology*, *7*(4), 727–750.

Nosek, B. A., Smyth, F. L., Sriram, N., Lindner, N. M., Devos, T., Ayala, A., Bar-Anan, Y., Bergh, R., Cai, H., Gonsalkorale, K., Kesebir, S., Maliszewski, N., Neto, F., Olli, E., Park, J., Schnabel, K., Shiomura, K., Tulbure, B. T., Wiers, R. W., Somogyi, M., Akrami, N., Ekehammar, B., Vianello, M., Banaji, M. R., & Greenwald, A. G. (2009). National differences in gender – science stereotypes predict national sex differences in sciences and math achievement. *Proceedings of the National Academy of Sciences of the United States of America*, *106*(26), 10593–10597.

O'Brien, M. & Huston, A. C. (1985). Development of sex-typed play behaviour in toddlers. *Developmental Psychology*, *21*(5), 866–871.

Öhrn, E. (1993). Gender, influence and resistance in school. *British Journal of Sociology of Education*, *14*(2), 147–158.

Olweus, D. (1991). Bully/victim problems among school children: Basic facts and effects of a school-based intervention program. In D. Peple & K. Rubin (Eds). *The development and treatment of childhood aggression* (pp. 411–448). Hillsdale, New Jersey: Lawrence Erlbaum.

ONS (2011). *Families and households in the UK, 2001 to 2010.* Retrieved from http://www.statistics.gov.uk/pdfdir/famhh0411.pdf

ONS & Department for Education (2011). *Teenage conception statistics for England 1998–2009.* Retrieved from http://media.education.gov.uk/assets/files/pdf/e/england%20under%2018%20and%20under%2016%20conception%20statistics%201998-2009%20feb%202011.pdf

Owens, L., Shute, R., & Slee, P. (2000). 'Guess what I just heard!': Indirect aggression among teenage girls in Australia. *Aggressive Behaviour*, *26*(1), 67–83.

Özkan, T. & Lajunen, T. (2005). Masculinity, femininity, and the Bem Sex Role Inventory in Turkey. *Sex Roles*, *52*(1/2), 103–110.

Palapattu, A. G., Kingery, J. N., & Ginsburg, G. S. (2006). Gender role orientation and anxiety symptoms among African American adolescents. *Journal of Abnormal Child Psychology*, *34*(3), 423–431.

Pande, R. P. (2003). Selective gender differences in childhood nutrition and immunization in rural India: The role of siblings. *Demography, 40*(3), 395–418.

Parkinson, B. (1995). *Ideas and realities of emotion.* London and New York: Routledge.

Patterson, M. L. & Werker, J. F. (2002). Infants' ability to match dynamic phonetic and gender information in the face and voice. *Journal of Experimental Child Psychology, 81*(1), 93–115.

Pavlov, I. P. (1927) (trans. G. V. Anrep). *Conditioned reflexes: An investigation of the physiological activity of the cerebral cortex.* London, England: Oxford University Press.

Pellegrini, A. D. (2006). The development and function of rough-and-tumble play in childhood and adolescence: A sexual selection theory perspective. In A. Göncü & S. Gaskins (Eds). *Play and development: Evolutionary, sociocultural and functional perspectives* (pp. 77–98). Mahwah, New Jersey: Lawrence Erlbaum Associates.

Pellegrini, A. D. & Long, J. D. (2002). A longitudinal study of bullying, dominance, and victimization during the transition from primary school through to secondary school. *British Journal of Developmental Psychology, 20*(2), 259–280.

Pellegrini, A. D. & Smith, P. K. (1998). Physical activity play: The nature and function of a neglected aspect of play. *Child Development, 69*(3), 577–598.

Peng, T. K. (2006). Construct validation of the Bem Sex Role Inventory in Taiwan. *Sex Roles, 55*(11/12), 843–851.

Penner, A. M. & Paret, M. (2008). Gender differences in mathematics achievement: Exploring the early grades and the extremes. *Social Science Research, 37*(1), 239–253.

Perry, D. G. & Bussey, K. (1979). The social learning theory of sex differences: Imitation is alive and well. *Journal of Personality and Social Psychology, 37*(10), 1699–1712.

Phillips, C. A., Rolls, S., Rouse, A., & Griffiths, M. D. (1995). Home video game playing in school children: A study of incidence and patterns of play. *Journal of Adolescence, 18*(6), 387–391.

Pierce, K. A. & Kirkpatrick, D. R. (1992). Do men lie on fear surveys? *Behaviour Research and Therapy, 30*(4), 415–418.

Pomerleau, A., Bolduc, D., Malcuit, G., & Cossette, L. (1990). Pink or blue: Environmental gender stereotypes in the first two years of life. *Sex Roles, 22*(5/6), 359–367.

Pompper, D. (2010). Masculinities, the metrosexual and media images: Across dimensions of age and ethnicity. *Sex Roles, 63*(9/10), 682–696.

Pooler, W. S. (1991). Sex of child preferences among college students. *Sex Roles, 25*(9/10), 569–576.

Pope, H. G., Olivardia, R., Gruber, A., & Borowiecki, J. (1999). Evolving ideals of male body image as seen through action toys. *International Journal of Eating Disorders, 26*(1), 65–72.

Potter, J. (1996). Discourse analysis and constructionist approaches: Theoretical background. In J. T. E. Richardson (Ed.). *Handbook of qualitative research methods for psychology and the social science*s (pp. 125–140). Leicester, England: BPS Books.

Poulin, F. & Pederson, S. (2007). Developmental changes in gender composition of friendship networks in adolescent girls and boys. *Developmental Psychology, 43*(6), 1484–1496.

Poulin-Dubois, D., Serbin, L. A., & Derbyshire, A. (1998). Toddlers' intermodal and verbal knowledge about gender. *Merrill-Palmer Quarterly, 44*(3), 338–354.

Poulin-Dubois, D., Serbin, L. A., Eichstedt, J. A., Sen, M. G., & Beissel, C. F. (2002). Men don't put on make-up: Toddler's knowledge of the gender stereotyping of household activities. *Social Development, 11*(2), 166–181.

Poulin-Dubois, D., Serbin, L. A., Kenyon, B., & Derbyshire, A. (1994). Infants intermodal knowledge about gender. *Developmental Psychology, 30*(3), 436–442.

Purvis, J. (2008). Sylvia Pankhurst (1882–1960), suffragette, political activist, artist and writer. *Gender and Education, 20*(1), 81–87.

Purvis, J. (2011). Emmeline Pankhurst (1858–1928), suffragette leader and single parent in Edwardian Britain. *Women's History Review, 20*(1), 87–108.

Ramirez, J. M. (2002). Hormones and aggression in childhood and adolescence. *Aggression and Violent Behavior, 8*(6), 621–644.

Reay, D. (2001). 'Spice girls', 'nice girls', 'girlies', and 'tomboys': Gender discourses, girls' cultures and femininities in the primary classroom. *Gender and Education, 13*(2), 153–166.

Reed, T. & Brown, M. (2000). The expression of care in the rough and tumble play of boys. *Journal of Research in Childhood Education, 15*(1), 104–116.

Remafedi, G. (1987). Adolescent homosexuality: Psychosocial and medical implications. *Pediatrics, 79*(3), 331–337.

Remafedi, G., Resnick, M., Blum, R., & Harris, L. (1992). Demography of sexual orientation in adolescents. *Pediatrics, 89*(4), 714–721.

Remafedi, G., French, S., Story, M. Resnick, M. D., & Blum, R. (1998). The relationship between suicide risk and sexual orientation: Results of a population-based study. *American Journal of Public Health, 88*(1), 57–60.

Rheingold, H. L. & Cook, K. V. (1975). The contents of boys' and girls' rooms as an index of parent's behaviour. *Child Development, 46*(2), 459–463.

Richardson, D. (2008). Conceptualizing gender. In D. Richardson & V. Robinson (Eds). *Introducing gender and women's studies*, 3rd Edition (pp. 3–19). Basingstoke and New York: Palgrave Macmillan.

Riviere, J. (1937) Love, hate and reparation: Two lectures. In M. Klein & J. Riviere (Eds). *Hate, greed and aggression* (pp. 1–53). London: Hogarth Press.

Robinson, J. P. & Lubienski, S. T. (2011). The development of gender achievement gaps in mathematics and reading during elementary and middle school: Examining direct cognitive assessments and teacher ratings. *American Educational Research Journal, 48*(2), 268–302.

Rose, A. J. & Montemayor, R. (1994). The relationship between gender role orientation and perceived self-competency in male and female adolescents. *Sex Roles, 31*(9/10), 579–595.

Rosenthal, T. L. & Bandura, A. (1978). Psychological modeling: Theory and practice. In S. L. Garfield & A. E. Bergin (Eds). *Handbook of psychotherapy and behaviour change: An empirical analysis*, 2nd Edition (pp. 621–658). New York: Wiley.

Rothbart, M. K., Ahadi, S. A., & Evans, D. E. (2000). Temperament and personality: Origins and outcomes. *Journal of Personality and Social Psychology, 78*(1), 122–135.

Rubin, J. Z., Provenzano, F. J., & Luria, Z. (1974). The eye of the beholder: Parents' views on sex of newborns. *American Journal of Orthopsychiatry, 44*(4), 512–519.

Russell, J. A. (1989). Culture, scripts, and children's understanding of emotion. In C. Saarni, & P. L. Harris (Eds). *Children's understanding of emotion* (pp. 293–318). Cambridge: Cambridge University Press.

Ryan, C., Huebner, D., Diaz, R. M., & Sanchez, J. (2009). Family rejection as a predictor of negative health outcomes in white and Latino lesbian, gay and bisexual young adults. *Pediatrics, 123*(1), 346–352.

Saenger, P. (1996). Turner's Syndrome. *The New England Journal of Medicine, 335*(23), 1749–1754.

Sandiford, P., Cassel, J., Montenegro, M., & Sanchez, G. (1995). The impact of women's literacy on child health and its interaction with access to health services. *Population Studies: A Journal of Demography, 49*(1), 5–17.

Sears, D. O. (1986). College sophomores in the laboratory: Influences of a narrow data base on social psychology's view of human nature. *Journal of Personality and Social Psychology, 51*(3), 515–530.

Serbin, L. A., Poulin-Dubois, D., & Eichstedt, J. A. (2002). Infants' responses to gender-inconsistent events. *Infancy, 3*(4), 531–542.

Serbin, L. A., Poulin-Dubois, D., Colburne, K. A., Sen, M. G., & Eichstedt, J. A. (2001). Gender stereotyping in infancy: Visual preferences for and knowledge of gender-stereotyped toys in the second year. *International Journal of Behavioral Development, 25*(1), 7–15.

Shakin, M., Shakin, D., & Sternglanz, S. H. (1985). Infant clothing: Sex labelling for strangers. *Sex Roles, 12*(9/10), 955–964.

Shankman, P. (1996). The history of Samoan sexual conduct and the Mead-Freeman controversy. *American Anthropologist, 98*(3), 555–567.

Shankman, P. (2000). Culture, biology, and evolution: The Mead-Freeman controversy revisited. *Journal of Youth and Adolescence, 29*(5), 539–556.

Shankman, P. (2009). *The trashing of Margaret Mead: Anatomy of an anthropological controversy.* Madison, Wisconsin: The University of Wisconsin Press.

Shanley, M. L. (1986). Suffrage, protective labor legislation, and married women's property laws in England. *Signs, 12*(1), 62–77.

Signorielli, N., McLeod, D., & Healy, E. (1994). Gender stereotypes in MTV commercials: The beat goes on. *Journal of Broadcasting and Electronic Media, 38*(1), 91–101.

Silverman, I. & Eals, M. (1992). Sex differences in spatial abilities: Evolutionary theory and data. In J. H. Barkow, L. Cosmides, & J. Tooby (Eds). *The adapted mind* (pp. 533–549). New York: Oxford University Press.

Silverman, I. & Philips, K. (1998). The evolutionary psychology of spatial sex differences. In C. Crawford & D. L. Krebs (Eds). *Handbook of evolutionary psychology* (pp. 595–612). Mahwah, NJ: Erlbaum.

Sisk, C. L. & Foster, D. L. (2004). The neural basis of puberty and adolescence. *Nature Neurosciences, 7*(10), 1040–1047.

Skinner, S. R., Smith, J., Fenwick, J., Hendriks, J., Fyfe, S., & Kendall, G. (2009). Pregnancy and protection: Perceptions, attitudes and experiences of Australian female adolescents. *Women and Birth, 22*(2), 50–56.

Slaby, R. G. & Frey, K. S. (1975). Development of gender constancy and selective attention to same-sex models. *Child Development, 46*(4), 849–856.

Slijper, F. M. E., Drop, S. L. S., Molenaar, J. C. & de Munick Keizer-Schrama, S. M. P. F. (1998). Long-term psychological evaluation of intersex children. *Archives of Sexual Behavior, 27*(2), 125–144.

Smith, C. & Lloyd, B. (1978). Maternal behaviour and perceived sex of infant: Revisited. *Child Development, 49*(4), 1263–1265.

Smith, P. K., Cowie, H., Olafsson, R. F., Liefooghe, A. P. D., Almeida, A., Araki, H., del Barrio, C., Costabile, A., Dekleva, B., Houndoumadi, A., Kim, K., Olajsson, R. P., Ortega, R., Pain, J., Pateraki, L., Schafer, M., Singer, M., Smorti, A., Toda, Y., Tomasson, H., & Wenxin, Z. (2002). Definitions of bullying: A comparison of terms used, and age and gender differences, in a fourteen-country international comparison. *Child Development, 73*(4), 1119–1133.

Smith, R. G. & Gross, A. M. (2006). Bullying: Prevalence and the effect of age and gender. *Child and Family Behavior Therapy, 28*(4), 13–37.

Solberg, M. E. & Olweus, D. (2003). Prevalence estimation of school bullying with the Olweus Bully/Victim Questionnaire. *Aggressive Behaviour, 29*(3), 239–268.

Spence, J. T. & Helmreich, R. L. (1981). Androgyny versus gender schema: A comment on Bem's gender schema theory. *Psychological Review, 88*(4), 365–368.

Spencer, S. J., Steele, C. M., & Quinn, D. M. (1999). Stereotype threat and women's math performance. *Journal of Experimental Social Psychology, 35*(1), 4–28.

Stacey, J. (2009). Unhitching the horse from the carriage: Love and marriage among the Mosuo. *Utah Law Review, 2*, 287–321.

Stam, H. J. (2001). Introduction: Social constructionism and its critics. *Theory and Psychology, 11*(3), 291–296.

Steensma, T. D., Biemond, R., de Boer, F., & Cohen-Kettenis, P. T. (2011). Desisting and persisting gender dysphoria after childhood: A qualitative follow-up study. *Clinical Child Psychology and Psychiatry*, DOI: 10.1177/1359104510378303. Retrieved from http://www.metamedicavumc.nl/pdfs/2011-01-07%20 genderdysphoria%20desisting%20and%20persisting.pdf

Stoneman, Z., Brody, G. H., & MacKinnon, C. E. (1986). Same-sex and cross-sex siblings: Activity choices, roles, behaviour, and gender stereotypes. *Sex Roles, 15*(9/10), 495–511.

Storr, A. (1989). *Freud.* New York and Oxford, England: Oxford University Press.

Strasburger, V. C. (2004). Children, adolescents, and the media. *Current Problems in Pediatric and Adolescent Health Care, 34*(2), 54–113.

Super, C. M., Axia, G., Harkness, S., Welles-Nyström, B., Zylicz, P. O., Parmar, P., Bonichini, S., Bermúdez, M. R., Moscardino, U., Kolar, V., Palacios, J., Eliasz, A., & McGurk, H. (2008). Culture, temperament, and the 'difficult child': A study in seven western cultures. *European Journal of Developmental Science, 2*(1/2), 136–157.

Swain, J. (2000). 'The money's good, the fame's good. The girls are good': The role of playground football in the construction of young boys' masculinity in a junior school. *British Journal of Sociology of Education, 21*(1), 95–109.

Tautner, H. M., Ruble, D. N., Cyphers, L., Kirsten, B., Behrendy, R., & Hartmann, P. (2005). Rigidity and flexibility of gender stereotypes in childhood: Developmental or differential? *Infant and Child Development, 14*(4), 365–382.

Thomas, A. & Chess, S. (1977). *Temperament and development.* New York: Brunner/Mazel.

Thompson, S. K. (1975). Gender labels and early sex role development. *Child Development, 46*(2), 339–347.

Tinklin, T. (2003). Gender differences and high attainment. *British Educational Research Journal, 29*(3), 307–325.

Toubia, N. (1994). Female circumcision as a public health issue. *The New England Journal of Medicine, 331*(11), 712–716.

Tripp, J. & Viner, R. (2005). Sexual health, contraception and teenage pregnancy. *British Medical Journal, 330*, 590–593.

Turner, H. H. (1938). A syndrome of infantilism, congential webbed neck and cubitus valgus. *Endocrinology, 28*(5), 566–574.

Turner-Bowker, D. M. (1996). Gender stereotyped descriptors in children's picture books: Does 'curious Jane' exist in the literature? *Sex Roles, 35*(7/8), 461–488.

Tymms, P., Merrell, C., & Henderson, B. (1997). The first year at school: A quantitative investigation of the attainment and progress of pupils. *Educational Research and Evaluation, 3*(2), 101–118.

UCAS (2011). *Gender: Applicant and accepted gender analysis over six year.* Retrieved from http://www.ucas.com/about_us/stat_services/stats_online/data_tables/gender, accessed 31 April 2011.

UNAIDS (2008). *Estimated number of children under 18 orphaned by AIDS in sub-Saharan Africa (1990–2007).* Retrieved from http://search2.unaids.org/custom/search.asp?IW_FIELD_WEB_STYLE=children+Africa&language=en& IW_INDEX=UNAIDS %20Documents&Start=1, accessed 2 May 2011.

UNAIDS (2010). *Fact sheet: Women, girls and HIV.* Retrieved from http://www.unaids.org/en/media/unaids/contentassets/dataimport/pub/factsheet/2010/20100302_fs_womenhiv_en.pdf, accessed 2 May 2011.

Unger, J. M. & Crawford, M. (1996). *Women and gender: A feminist approach.* New York: McGraw Hill.

Upton, R. L. (2003). 'Women have no tribe': Connecting carework, gender, and migration in an era of HIV/AIDS in Botswana. *Gender & Society, 17*(2), 314–322.

Urberg, K. A., Değirmenicioğlu, S. M., Tolson, J. M., & Halliday-Scher, K. (1995). The structure of adolescent peer networks. *Developmental Psychology, 31*(4), 540–547.

Valentine, G. (1997). 'My son's a bit dizzy.' 'My wife's a bit soft': Gender, children and cultures of parenting. *Gender, Place and Culture, 4*(1), 37–62.

Vasey, P. L. & Bartlett, N. H. (2007). What can the Samoan 'Fa'afafine' teach us about the Western concept of gender identity disorder in childhood? *Perspectives in Biology and Medicine, 50*(4), 481–490.

Vasey, P. L., Pocock, D. S., & Vanderlaan, D. P. (2007). Kind selection and male androphilia in Samoan *fa'afafine. Evolution and Human Behavior, 28*(3), 159–167.

Verma, R. K., Pulerwitz, J., Mahendra, V., Khandekar, S., Barker, G., Fulpagare, P., & Singh, S. K. (2006). Challenging and changing gender attitudes among young men in Mumbai, India. *Reproductive Health Matters, 14*(28), 135–143.

Vygotsky, L. (1978). *Mind in society: The development of higher psychological processes.* Cambridge, MA: Harvard University Press.

Vygotsky, L. (1986) (A. Kozulin, trans.). *Thought and Language.* Cambridge, Massachusetts: MIT Press.

Vygotsky, L. (1998). *Collected works: Volume 5.* New York: Plenum.

Walkerdine, V., Lucey, H., & Melody, J. (2002). *Growing up girl: Psychosocial explorations of gender and class.* London: Palgrave Macmillan.

Ward, C. & Sethi, R. R. (1986). Cross-cultural validation of the Bem Sex Role Inventory. *Journal of Cross-Cultural Psychology, 17*(3), 300–314.

Warwick, I., Aggeleton, P., & Douglas, N. (2001). Playing it safe: Addressing the emotional and physical health of lesbian and gay pupils in the U.K. *Journal of Adolescence, 24*(1), 129–140.

Watson, J. B. (1913). Psychology as the behaviourist views it. *Psychological Review, 20*(2), 158–177.

Weisner, T. S. (1996). Why ethnography should be the most important method of study in human development. In R. A. Shweder (Ed.). *Ethnography and human development: Context and meaning in social inquiry* (pp. 305–324). Chicago & London: University of Chicago Press.

Weiss, E., Wehaln, D., & Gupta, G. R. (2000). Gender, sexuality and HIV: Making a difference in the lives of young women in developing countries. *Sexual and Relationship Therapy, 15*(3), 233–245.

Werner-Wilson, R. J. (1998). Gender differences in adolescent sexual attitudes: The influences of individual and family factors. *Adolescence, 33*(131), 519–531.

West, C. & Zimmerman, D. H. (1983). Small insults: A study of interruptions in cross-sex conversations between unacquainted persons. In B. Thorne, C. Kramarae, & N. Henley (Eds). *Language, gender and society* (pp. 102–117). Rowley, Massachusetts: Newbury House Publishers.

Whincup, P. H., Gilg, J. A., Odoki, K., Taylor, S. J. C., & Cook, D. G. (2001). Age of menarche in contemporary British teenagers: Survey of girls born between 1982 and 1986. *British Medical Journal, 322,* 1095–1096.

Wilcox, C. & Francis, L. J. (1997). Beyond gender stereotyping: Examining the validity of the Bem Sex Role Inventory among 16- to 19-year old females in England. *Personality and Individual Differences, 23*(1), 9–13.

Wilson, D., McMaster, J., Greenspan, R., Mboyi, L., Ncuube, T., & Sibanda, B. (1990). Cross-cultural validation of the Bem Sex Role Inventory in Zimbabwe. *Personality and Individual Differences, 11*(7), 651–656.

Wilson, P., Sharp, C., & Carr, S. (1999). The prevalence of gender dysphoria in Scotland: A primary care study. *British Journal of General Practice, 49*(449), 991–992.

Wiseman, C. V., Gray, J. J., Mosimann, J. E., & Ahrens, A. H. (1992). Cultural expectations of thinness in women: An update. *International Journal of Eating Disorders, 11*, 85–89.

Wolff, C. G. (1979). Erickson's 'inner space' reconsidered. *Massachusetts Review, 20*(2), 355–368.

Woodfield, R., Earl-Novell, S., & Solomon, L. (2005). Gender and mode of assessment at university: Should we assume female students are better suited to coursework and males to unseen examinations? *Assessment and Evaluation in Higher Education, 30*(1), 35–50.

World Health Organisation (2010a). *HIV/AIDS: Data and statistics*. Retrieved from http://www.who.int/hiv/data/en/index.html

World Health Organisation (2010b). *Paediatric HIV data and statistics*. Retrieved from http://www.who.int/hiv/topics/paediatric/data/en/index1.html

World Health Organization (2011). *Female genital mutilation and other harmful practices: Prevalence of FGM*. Retrieved from http://www.who.int/reproductivehealth/topics/fgm/prevalence/en/index.html, accessed 16 September 2011.

Yonkers, K. A., O'Brien, P. M. S., & Erkisson, E. (2008). Premenstrual Syndrome. *The Lancet, 371*(9619), 1200–1210.

Young, I. M. (1980). Throwing like a girl: A phenomenology of feminine body comportment motility and spatiality. *Human Studies, 3*(1), 137–156.

Younger, M., Warrington, M., & Williams, J. (1999). The gender gap and classroom interactions: Reality or rhetoric? *British Journal of Sociology of Education*, 20(3), 325-341.

Zammichieli, M. E., Gilroy, F. D., & Sherman, M. F. (1988). Relation between sex-role orientation and marital satisfaction. *Personality and Social Psychology Bulletin, 14*(4), 747–754.

Zhou, J.-N., Hofman, M. A., Gooren, L. J., & Swaab, D. F. (1995). A sex difference in the human brain and its relation to transsexuality. *Nature, 378*, 68–70.

Zimmer-Gembeck, M. J. & Helfand, M. (2008). Ten years of longitudinal research on U. S. adolescent sexual behaviour: Developmental correlates of sexual intercourse, and the importance of age, gender and ethnic background. *Developmental Review, 28*(2), 153–224.

Zucker, K. J. (2005). Gender identity disorder in children and adolescents. *Annual Review of Clinical Psychology, 1*(1), 467–492.

Zucker, K. J. & Cohen-Kettenis, P. T. (2008). Gender identity disorder in children and adolescents. In D. L. Rowland & L. Incrocci (Eds). *Handbook of sexual and gender identity disorders* (pp. 376–422). Hoboken, New Jersey: John Wiley & Sons. Inc.

Index

Note: Entries in **bold** refer to glossary definitions

Reading guide

This table identifies where in the book you'll find relevant information for those of you studying or teaching A-level. You should also, of course, refer to the Index and the Glossary, but navigating a book for a particular set of items can be awkward and we found this table a useful tool when editing the book and so include it here for your convenience.

TOPIC	AQA(A)	AQA(B)	EDEXCEL	PAGE
Cognitive development theory	x	x		86
Kohlberg	x	x		86
Gender schema theory	x			94
Hormones	x		x	8
Genes	x		x	5
Evolutionary explanations	x		x	11
Biosocial approach	x			15
Gender dysphoria	x			17
Influence of parents	x			31
Influence of peers	x			46
Influence of schools	x			46
Influence of media	x			54–55, 104
Cultural influences	x			147
Nature/nurture		x	x	13
Social learning theory		x	x	111
Androgyny		x		96
Sex-role stereotypes		x		102
Turner's syndrome		x		6
Androgen influence		x	x	9
Gender identity		x		87
Gender stability		x		88
Gender constancy		x		88
Psychoanalytic theory		x	x	70
Oedipus complex		x	x	76
Electra complex		x	x	77